The Wicked West

The Wicked West

Boozers, Cruisers, Gamblers, and More

Sherry Monahan

Rio Nuevo Publishers
Tucson, Arizona

For two special people in my writing life ...
The late Carl Chafin—a mentor and friend. He was the first person to
freely offer his resources, time, and knowledge. Without Carl, my first
book, Taste of Tombstone, *would not have been possible. Rest in peace.*
And Bob Boze Bell—a "True West" friend and all around good guy. After
reading my work several years ago, Bob became an instant supporter and
friend. His wit, charm, and willingness to help never cease to amaze me.

RIO NUEVO PUBLISHERS®
P.O. Box 5250, Tucson, Arizona 85703-0250
(520) 623-9558, www.rionuevo.com

Library of Congress Cataloging-in-Publication Data

Monahan, Sherry A.
  The wicked West : boozers, cruisers, gamblers, and more / Sherry Monahan.
    p. cm.
  Includes bibliographical references.
  ISBN-13: 978-1-887896-74-0
  ISBN-10: 1-887896-74-0
  1. West (U.S.)--Social life and customs--19th century. 2. Bars (Drinking establishments)--West (U.S.)--History--19th century. 3. Gambling--West (U.S.)--History--19th century. 4. Drinking of alcoholic beverages--West (U.S.)--History--19th century. 5. Prostitution--West (U.S.)--History--19th century. I. Title.

F596.M654 2005
978'.02--dc22

2005013318

Design: Dawn DeVries Sokol
Front cover design: Larry Lindahl (image courtesy of Library of Congress, #CPH 3A22178).

Printed in the United States of America.

10   9   8   7   6   5   4   3   2

Contents

Foreword

My old *compadre* Bob Boze Bell, who knows more than anyone should about the Wicked West both past and present, is one of Sherry Monahan's biggest fans. When I began preparations for the interviews for a 2004 television documentary on the O.K. Corral that I was co-producing with Bill Kurtis for the History Channel, Bell gave me the hard sell on Ms. Monahan as a perfect talking head for the production. Bruce Dinges kindly arranged for the filming to take place at the Arizona Historical Society museum, where the author of *Taste of Tombstone* (1998) was placed amidst a pioneer store exhibit. Bell was dead right, as he surprisingly often is, for Sherry Monahan brought just the right combination of wit, knowledge, and grace to her interview and to our television show.

Once I met her and realized her absolute passion for the story of the American West, and especially its day-to-day rhythms and its people both forgotten and famous, I could see why Bell was so smitten. She was dedicated to getting at the beating heart of everyday frontier life. Her goal was to not only perfectly re-create living conditions from the distant past but also make them comprehensible to the rest of us in the harried present.

Her enthusiasm for the West has led her and her husband, Larry, to buy a ranch not far from Tombstone, Arizona. There they can soak in the Western environment in all its harsh splendor, drawing inspiration from one of the grandest and starkest landscapes in America. Her love of this land and its rich past comes across in every page of her writing. This passion for her subject is downright contagious, as you the reader will soon come to more fully understand as you proceed on with this book.

So join Sherry Monahan on a journey back in time to a place she knows so very well. Enter the saloons, theaters, and bawdy houses, both grand and austere, and learn how folks entertained themselves in the Wild West. In this journey you will discover that people are pretty much the same across time and space, although their entertainments have certainly dramatically changed. Still, you will find some amazing common ground between past and present, all nimbly presented by your delightful hostess on this historical journey. No one knows this pioneer territory better than Sherry Monahan. But watch out—her passion for the Wicked West is contagious.

Paul Andrew Hutton
Professor of History, University of New Mexico

Introduction

This book will take you back to a place and time where whiskey, gambling, and money ruled. This is a book that offers readers an inside glimpse into the Wild West—and it was wild indeed. The men and women who made their homes here worked hard and played just as hard. Step into a saloon and belly up to the bar for a little coffin varnish or jig juice. Take a spin around the dance floor with a sporting woman or wager with a tinhorn gambler. Become a saloon mixologist and whip up a drink recipe from a popular Western saloon, or learn to "buck the tiger" as you play a saloon banking game.

In these pages, the voices and vices of the Wild West come alive. Their tales are authentic. I hope you'll discover, as I did, that life in the nineteenth-century West wasn't all cowpokes and gunslingers. It had a lively culture, an astonishing diversity, and even a language all its own. What we have come to think of as the "vice" or "wicked" aspects of frontier life was largely a judgment imposed by the Victorian standards of the day and the strict Christian mores of the churches of the time. By today's standards, life in the West was always unpredictable, often rough, and sometimes dangerous. Yet saloons, gamblers, and sporting women offered Westerners more than just the opportunity to spend money, bend the rules, or indulge themselves—in so many ways they proved an important asset to the social life, the economy, and the building of the West into the thriving, lively, and diverse area it remains to this day. So join me in a guided tour back into the wild days when the West made history. Cheers!

Chapter 1

Come Hell or Firewater:

The Saloons

WHEN PEOPLE ENVISION THE HEROES AND VIL-
LAINS of the Wild West, they're usually walking into or
out of a saloon. Once news of a new boomtown or cow
town was out, a saloon was often the first business to open its doors,
usually due to the basic laws of supply and demand. Life was often
rough in a new town, and there was little to do after work but drink
and chat at the local watering hole. Saloons, often one of the first
places to open in a town or camp, saw some of the liveliest times in
the West. From high-stake games to shady ladies and gunfights,
saloons continued to boom in their respective towns until Prohibition.

Up until then, the vices pursued in saloons across the Old West
were as varied as the barrooms where they thrived, but each offered
the basics. A traveler riding into a new town could be assured of a
place to rest, libation, and something to eat—all for the right price.

When most of us think of saloons in a wild, Western town, we
think of loud bawdy places, filled with rough characters, cancan girls,
and cheap whiskey. And while that was sometimes true, many saloons
were pretty basic, consisting of a bar, spittoons, glassware, some gaming tables, and liquor. Yet there were just as many upscale drinking
establishments, especially in Colorado, California, Nevada, and
Arizona, that barely resembled their rough and ready counterparts.

Sometimes the bar was deserted in favor of the saloon's gaming tables.

These were places where sophisticated businessmen, hard-working miners, and high-stake gamblers made up the clientele, and the atmosphere was usually far from bawdy. Upscale saloons were elaborately decorated, and their keepers sold the finest liquors, champagne, wine, and cigars that could be procured.

Many saloons, of course, did start out rough. They were set up in tents, had minimal supplies, and offered less than palatable liquor. But as they prospered, saloons rapidly grew into sophisticated meccas where gentlemen sought relief from the daily grind. There they discussed business and politics while enjoying their favorite libations and cigars at the bar. Though many saloons became more or less respectable, respectable women were not among the customers. Victorian standards (not to mention double standards) were the order of the day, and most women wouldn't dare frequent such establishments—it was just not proper. Nor did men want them there; the barroom was a place where men could seek solace among their brethren. The only women to be found were either waitresses or the occasional solo singer. On occasion, women dealt faro, but this was the exception rather than the rule. Saloons were mostly owned by men, but some were actually run by women. Many of these establishments were referred to as "dance houses" or "dance halls" and generally frequented by less-than-respectable women or "soiled doves." Here was where female "hostesses" or "queens" plied their trade.

While larger, wealthier towns tended to be home to sophisticated social clubs, they had their share of dance halls and hole-in-the-wall places, too. Smaller, remote towns usually had a few basic saloons, and some doubled as a social hotspot because of their locale. Women in those towns might enter without fear for their reputations, but this was not the norm across the West. According to Tucson, Arizona, pioneer C. C. Wheeler, "A woman was seldom seen in a saloon and, in fact, the only time women appeared where gambling was conducted, or liquor sold, was during Fiesta season."

Most establishments did not have tables or chairs in the main saloon area, though some did offer a few card tables or reading tables in the back. In sophisticated cities such as Virginia City, Nevada, and Tombstone, Arizona, saloons were different from those in other towns, because they served rich mining communities and not rough cow towns. Yet even some of the cow town saloons were nicely

---

Gin Sling
(Use a water glass)

1 teaspoon sugar, dissolved in
  a little water
1 jigger of Holland gin
Water

Place ingredients in the glass, and fill up balance with water. Stir with a spoon, grate a little nutmeg on top, and serve. Add a slice of lemon if the customer desires it.

decorated and carried fine liquors and cigars. Though it's true that sometimes drunken cowhands would shoot at the glassware stacked behind the bar, or shoot out the lights, it was often the case that, once sober, the culprits would return to the scene of their crimes, apologize to the owner, and ask to pay for the damages.

In a small town, saloon patrons likely found the basics—a bartender, glasses, tables, spittoons, and alcohol. However, in a bigger, wealthier town, saloons were elaborately decorated with mahogany, oil paintings, chandeliers, and expensive carpets. An endless supply of the highest quality whiskey, champagne, cordials, rum, wine, and more could be had. There was usually a reading section that carried newspapers from around the country, as well as other periodicals. A saloon often had a small cigar concession near the front entrance.

A high Victorian example of a "toney" establishment.

This way, both male and female patrons could make purchases without actually entering the saloon.

Alcohol aside, saloons drew crowds because they offered gambling. Gambling concessions and cigar stands were housed in many saloons, and someone other than the saloon owners often ran them. Faro dealers would bring in their equipment and set up shop, and saloon owners allowed it since the gaming was a good way to draw in the crowds. In addition, they received a portion of the profits. Most saloons offered a separate section for poker, usually in the back. But most of the time, it was a far cry from the old Hollywood image of a secluded, smoke-filled room where a bunch of desperadoes were ready to kill one another over a hand of cards. It is true a gambler could get shot over a game of cards, but only if he were caught cheating. The most popular saloon games were faro, monte, keno, and poker, but occasionally gamblers enjoyed other games of the time such as roulette and twenty-one. Men also played dominoes, cribbage, and euchre.

Owning a saloon was one of the most profitable professions in the Old West. It could also be highly respectable. In Virginia City, Nevada, home of the Comstock Mining District, a man could make a grand living as a saloon owner. This thriving silver-mining community was founded in 1859 and was one of the most prosperous mining towns in American history. Even Samuel Clemens, a.k.a. Mark Twain, called it home. In 1847, he was apprenticed to a printer and wrote for his brother's newspaper. After a brief career as a steamboat pilot, he moved in 1862 to Virginia City, where he edited the *Territorial Enterprise.* There on February 3, 1863, a new writer was born when Clemens published his first story using the name "Mark Twain."

In *Roughing It,* he described Virginia City as the "livest town, for its age and population, that America had ever produced." He painted this vivid picture of a street scene:

> The sidewalks swarmed with people.... The streets
> themselves were just as crowded with quartz wagons, freight

> ## Whiskey Cocktail
>
> ¾ glass of shaved ice
> 1 or 2 dashes curaçao
> 2 or 3 dashes of gum syrup (or substitute sugar syrup, which is equal parts water and sugar heated together until clear)
> 1 jigger of whiskey
> 1½–2 dashes of bitters
>
> Stir up well with a spoon and strain it in a cocktail glass, putting in a cherry or a medium-sized olive, and squeeze a piece of lemon peel on the top, and serve. This is without a doubt one of the most popular American drinks in existence.

teams, and other vehicles. The procession was endless. So great was the pack, that buggies frequently had to wait half an hour for an opportunity to cross the principal street. Joy sat on every countenance, and there was a glad, almost fierce, intensity in every eye, that told of the money-getting schemes that were seething in every brain and the high hope that held sway in every heart. Money was as plenty as dust; every individual considered himself wealthy, and a melancholy countenance was nowhere to be seen.

Half serious and half satirical, Twain went on to suggest that in Virginia City "the cheapest way to become an influential man and be looked upon by the community at large was to stand behind a bar, wear a cluster diamond pin, and sell whiskey." He went on: "I am not sure but that the saloonkeeper had a shade higher rank than any other member of society. His opinion had weight ...."

Twain wasn't the only one writing about Virginia City—as a large mining town, it made the news in just about every part of the country. In 1860, *The Sacramento Union* painted this memorable picture of one of the local watering holes:

Little stacks of gold and silver fringed from the monte tables and glittered beneath the swinging lamps. A ceaseless din of boisterous talk, oaths, and laughter spread from the open doors into the streets. The rattle of dice, coin, balls, and spinning markers, flapping greasy cards, and a chorus of calls and interjections went on day and night, while clouds of tobacco smoke filled the air and blacked the roof timbers, modifying the stench rising from the stained and greasy floors, soiled clothes, and hot flesh of the unwashed company.

❧ HIGH LIVING IN VIRGINIA CITY ❧

All was bustle and hurry, noise, excitement, and confusion. The ... saloons were crowded with men in huge overcoats, the pockets of which were filled with big specimens, small silver bars, and rolls of location notices and assay certificates, buying, selling, and talking mines, and "bummers" of the seediest class, who drank at the expense of every stranger who approached the bar—swore, talked, fought, and "swapped" filthy lies from morning to night.

In the evening the streets were deserted, but the mad excitement indoors was as great as ever. The bartenders were kept in incessant motion in their frantic efforts to supply the demand for drinks, which poured in from every direction .... The dance house was filled with tipsy miners, with a sprinkling of abandoned women, whose smiles and favors were as eagerly sought for and as jealously observed by the unfavored as were those of the most gifted and virtuous of their sex in the abode of wealth and refinement, at the East, on a gala night.

In the rear of every barroom was a door bearing a sign inscribed "Club Room," through which was heard the strains of discordant music and the chinking of coin. These club rooms were crowded to their utmost capacity, and the tables were piled with coin and checks, while hundreds of men, who had made lucky strikes at finding, work-ing, or, more frequently, selling mines, were betting away in a single hour what might have kept them, and those dependent on them, for years in comfort, or served as the foundation for a colossal fortune. Every five or ten minutes the dealers would pause in their work of turning cards and raking down the coin to ring a bell, when a bar-tender would enter the club room. "Gentlemen, what will you take? You drink with me, you know!" said the smiling dealer in pasteboard and other people's hard-earned coin. "Whiskey toddy! Whiskey straight! Whiskey hot! Whiskey sour! Whiskey and gum!" replied the crowd; the fiery liquor was swallowed, and the game went on ...."

Excerpted from: Overland Monthly, *March 1869*

The cattle business was more stable and predictable than mining, and thousands of cowboys shared the quintessential Western experience of riding into new towns after months on the trail. The dusty civilization of these outposts looked opulent after hard earth beds and the company of cattle. In Texas, cowhands were known as "waddies," and their needs were well understood. One pioneer Texas resident, Richard Murphy, remembered their forays into the cow town of Amarillo in the late 1800s. "Amarillo was a pure cow town those days and run by stage. There were just a few women folks in the town, and they were at premium. Most of the waddies would make the town after the roundup, and some of the boys would stay there until all their money was gone."

Jack Hull, a resident of Texico, New Mexico, remembered his first experience of a cow town with the wide-eyed amazement of a boy: "More or less fascinated by the wide-open aspect of the town, with its saloons, dance halls, and gambling places, I strolled down the board sidewalk and dropped into one of the saloons. Frontier nightlife was in full swing in the place. Men gambled at tables, a dance was in progress in the rear of the place, and around the bar

---

Mint Julep

½ cup sugar
½ cup water
Fresh mint leaves
Crushed ice
Bourbon

Cook the sugar and water in a saucepan over medium heat until sugar has completely dissolved. Place several mint leaves in a non-breakable container, and pour the sugar syrup over the leaves. Refrigerate for at least 4 hours.

Fill tumbler glasses with crushed ice. Add 3 parts of sugar water to 1 part bourbon. If this is too sweet for one's taste, adjust the proportions of sugar water and bourbon. A little water can also be added. Garnish with a sprig of fresh mint. Makes about 2 drinks.

stood booted and spurred cowpunchers evidently in town to celebrate after long weeks on the range. I stopped just inside the door [and] was taking in the sight when a big cowhand walked over to the bar and, with a sweeping beckon of his arm, yelled, 'the drinks are on me. Come on up.' Men left the game tables and all strolled to the bar for the courtesy drink, which such an offer meant. Unaccustomed to the etiquette of the West, I remained where I stood near the door, and the host of the

---

Gin Toddy
(Use a whiskey glass)

½ teaspoon sugar, dissolved in a
  little water
1 or 2 lumps of crushed ice
1 jigger of Holland gin

Stir well, and serve. The proper way to serve this drink is to dissolve the sugar with a little water, put the spoon and ice into the glass, and hand out the bottle of liquor to the customer to help himself.

---

drinks spotted me. 'Say, ain't you gonna drink on me?' he asked, with his face in a scowl. 'No, thanks,' I replied, 'I don't care for anything,' and with that I thought the matter was dismissed. But it wasn't. 'So you won't drink on me?' he asked as he started towards me. I began to realize that something was about to happen when the bartender came to my rescue. He stepped from behind the bar, and taking the irked cowhand by the arm he said, 'That's just a kid. You don't want to make a kid drink on you.' The irritated cowhand walked a little closer to me for a better appraisal of my age, I suppose, then he turned back to the bar with a wave of his arm that apparently dismissed the incident. It is needless to say that I left with my first lesson in frontier etiquette well-learned and a wholesome respect for a gentlemen of the range when they turn host at the bar."

While saloons may have varied in style and variety throughout the West, they basically served the same purposes—drinking, discussing business and politics, and gambling. Inside, saloon interiors ranged from simple to elegant. Very few had the swinging doors you see in the movies. Can you imagine the dust and dirt rolling in from the streets had there been swinging doors? Most had typical fourteen-foot double doors, like other Victorian-style buildings. Some saloons did have a set of swinging doors, but they were often installed beyond the first set of bigger doors.

Tombstone started out in an unlikely patch of southern Arizona where water and lumber were scarce, but it quickly turned into a town bustling with miners, businessmen, gamblers, and cowboys. Exploding in population from its founding in 1879, the town rapidly grew to be one of the most famous boomtowns in the history of the West, with saloons to match. The Alhambra saloon was one of the finest of its time. The center of the saloon contained a large Gothic chair with velvet and Morocco upholstery in which the "ruling spirit sat on his throne to watch over" his saloon. On both sides were bar fixtures made of walnut, mahogany, and rosewood. They were adorned with wrought and filigree work, neatly gilded and finished. There were extravagant sets of Bohemian, Italian, and French glassware with splendid designs and patterns. The bar stock was expansive and included the finest drinks, the best liquor, the choicest imported wines, brandies, liqueurs, and cigars. The *Tombstone Nugget* proudly proclaimed that "the mass of people ... can support anything that is truly bon ton and tony."

Not to be outdone, Tombstone's other entrepreneurs made sure their establishments remained competitively upscale. The Oriental Saloon had different owners over the years, but when Milton Joyce & Co. opened its doors on July 21, 1880, the *Tombstone Epitaph* reported this "soon to be famous" establishment was the most elegantly furnished saloon "this side of the Golden Gate." The *Epitaph* reporter gave a detailed description of the rooms:

Twenty-eight burners suspended in neat chandeliers afforded an illumination of ample brilliancy, and the bright rays reflected from many colored crystals on the bar sparkled like a December iceling in the sunshine .... The saloon comprised two apartments. To the right of the main entrance is the bar, beautifully carved, finished in white gilt and capped with a handsomely polished top. In the rear of this stand a brace of sideboards, which are simply elegant and must be seen to be appreciated. They were made for the Baldwin Hotel, of San Francisco, but being too small, Mr. Joyce purchased them. The back apartment is covered with brilliant Brussels carpet, and suitably furnished after the style of a grand club room, with conveniences for the wily dealers in polished ivory. The selection of furniture and fixtures displays an exquisite taste, and nothing seems to have been forgotten—even a handsome stock of stationery.

Presiding over the bar was Johnny Chenowith. He didn't just pour Rock and Rye whiskey into a glass; he created wonderful specialty drinks such as Brandy Smashes, A.V.H. Gins, and Russian Cocktails. The Oriental even attracted the Tombstone Glee Club, which began rehearsing there in late July. Two months later, patrons were serenaded by pianist Charley Willoughby, while former Tucson caterer Isaac "Little Jakey" Jacobs provided patrons with fresh

---

Whiskey Punch

Juice of ½ lemon
2 ounces whiskey
1 teaspoon sugar
1 dash brandy

Shake all ingredients together. Strain into a glass or goblet that has been filled with shaved or crushed ice. Garnish with fruit.

oysters, shrimp, and crabs imported from San Francisco. It's known that Wyatt Earp had a faro table in the Oriental during his stay in Tombstone.

Tombstone's saloons were impressive, even for those used to larger cities in California. Newly relocated from San Diego to Tombstone, Arizona, intrepid journalist Clara Brown wrote:

> Saloon openings are all the rage. The Oriental is simply gorgeous and is pronounced the finest place of the kind this side of San Francisco. The bar is a marvel of beauty; the sideboards were made for the Baldwin Hotel; the gaming room connected is carpeted with Brussels; brilliantly lighted, and furnished with reading matter and writing materials for its patrons. Every evening music from the piano and violin attracts a crowd; and the scene is really a gay one—but for all the men. To be sure, there are frequent dances, which I have heard called, "respectable," but so long as so many members of the *demimonde* who are numerous and very showy here patronize them, many honest women will hesitate to attend.

The owners of the Grand Hotel on Allen Street built the Fountain Saloon under the hotel around September 1882. Since the mines ran underneath Tombstone and Allen Streets, the miners only had a short walk to unwind after a hard day's work. Misters Alderson and Gratton ran the place and offered imported beer on draught and in bottles. They also offered imported lunches, liquors, and cigars.

Tombstone happens to be well documented, but similar accounts survive from other Western locales. Pioneer J. R. Irving of Oswego, Oregon, recalled saloon life in the 1870s. "Do I know anything about the old White 'Ouse, down on the river?" he said. "Why damn it, o' course I do. I know all them fellers that went out there. Everybody that 'ad a fast horse—and all the bloods 'ad fast horses in them days—drove out the old Macadam Road along the river to the White 'Ouse. It 'ad wide porches, out over the river, and a body could get most anything to drink."

According to Irving, the White House offered opportunities for many types of misbehavior: "They used to say that was where a man took another man's wife. Then if he found out some way his wife wus there with mebbe the husband of the woman with 'im, 'e'd drive around the 'alf-mile racetrack an' go back to town, as good

> ### Applejack
> *(Use a large bar glass)*
>
> ¾ glass of shaved ice
> 2 or 3 dashes of gum syrup *(do not use too much)*
> 1½–2 dashes of bitters
> 1 or 2 dashes of curaçao
> 1 jigger of applejack
>
> Stir up well with a spoon and strain into a cocktail glass. Put in a cherry or medium-sized olive; squeeze a piece of lemon peel on top and serve. This is a popular and palatable drink.

as you please. That's what they said, an' that you could hev just about anything you wanted at the White 'Ouse, besides fine food and champagne ...."

A saloon near Coeur d'Alene, Idaho, was locally famous in its own way. In 1883, the *Idaho Statesman* published a story—or review of local entertainment possibilities—entitled "The Coeur d'Alene Saloonist," which began, "Eagle City is located in the forks of Prichard and Eagle creeks. It has more saloons and faro games than you can shake a stick at. The stock in trade consists of a sack of flour for a bar, a bottle of coffin varnish, a bucket of water, and two sized glasses."

Sometimes just walking into a saloon could be deadly. On March 9, 1890, the *Black Hills Daily Times* in the Dakota Territory reported, "W. B. King, well-known character of Central, entered saloon and, taking a seat at a table, immediately expired."

The Wicked West

As late as 1903, saloons were still a dangerous place in some towns. *The Dallas Morning Star* reported a daring holdup in New Mexico by three masked bandits. The three entered a saloon in Santa Rita in September 1903 around midnight. Heavily armed, they rode up to the Miner's Exchange saloon, which was owned by W. H. Ernest. When they asked for a drink, the proprietor arose from bed to wait upon them. Once inside the saloon, the bandits drew their guns and threatened the owner with his life if he did not open his safe. Then, when Ernest opened the door, they locked him in an adjoining room and rifled through the safe, stealing more than $600 in cash. Sheriff Blair of Silver City was notified and began pursuit immediately, but it is uncertain whether the bandits were eventually captured.

As saloons multiplied and their prices rose, many of them began offering luxury services to attract wealthy customers. A popular trend of the time was for a saloon to serve free lunches to its patrons. The food not only attracted customers, but also made them thirsty! The typical menu offered pickled herring, roast beef, roast turkey, pickled eggs, sardines, and olives, and one even offered *pâté de foie grois*. The period's bartenders' guides favored quality over quantity, though not everyone followed that rule. Some saloons hired caterers to supervise and prepare the free lunch.

Saloons often chose their menus based on the ethnicity of their customers. While German patrons might have appreciated sauerkraut and bologna, someone of French or Irish descent may have sauntered to the next saloon for different fare, as well as the company of someone from their homeland.

Food was only part of the saloon experience, and most saloons found ways to bring more luxury to the bar as well as the restaurant. Some bartenders provided their customers with a bar-spoon. This was suggested for the very sophisticated customer who wore gloves, since removing the gloves might have proved difficult. The spoon was provided so the customer could dip out the fruit that accompanied most fancy

The sheer variety of mixed drinks also required the saloonkeeper to have an array of drink glasses, including champagne, wine, whiskey, brandy snifters, and cordials. (Glasses courtesy of Tombstone Western Heritage Museum.)

drinks of the time. The sheer variety of mixed drinks also required the saloonkeeper to have an array of drink glasses, including champagne, wine, whiskey, brandy snifters, and cordials. In addition, there were glasses for beer, which included sizes from a small glass to a big schooner.

Saloons also offered a wide variety of entertainment besides food and gambling. Many saloons serenaded their patrons with music, which might range from brass bands to string quartets, pianists, and more. The music played in saloons was not the stereotypical 1860s "Camptown Races" or "Oh Susannna" pounded out by a drunken cowboy. Some saloon owners hired professional singers to add to the establishment's ambiance, including regular performances by singers and stars of the day. One former actor found his way to Phoenix,

Arizona, in the late 1800s, and in 1889 put together a banjo player, guitarist, and violinist to form a vaudeville act. They took their show to the popular Blue Bird saloon, and combined music with stunts and comic songs to amuse the crowds night after night.

Showmen in bigger Western towns often put together a variety theater, and any number of national celebrities toured the West. The theater's owner usually had a regular troupe of actors and performers on his payroll, but he also booked traveling acts. When a troupe came to town, the owner might lay off his regular entertainers or send them to another town to perform. The troupes, mainly women, consisted of song-and-dance teams, singing, and specialty acts. These dancers were a cut above the "dance hall girls." For the most part, they wore modest costumes, and while their dresses were considered short, one rarely saw bare legs. Some of the performers were stars in their particular line, while others were just waitresses trying to earn a living. Since a large part of their pay was based on the percentage of drinks they sold during the night, they also served drinks to patrons in the box seats or to anyone else who may have asked. Sometimes customers would invite the girls to join them for a drink. As they did not want to become intoxicated between performances, the bartender would often pour them tea as a substitute for whiskey.

As families moved West to join their husbands, fathers, and brothers, Western towns became more and more "civilized." In Tombstone, respectable entertainment quickly found an audience. Citizens were proud of their progress and, near the close of 1881, *The Epitaph* wrote:

> ### As families moved West to join their husbands, fathers, and brothers, Western towns became more and more "civilized."

It is safe to say that no other town in America, of its size and population, is better supplied in the way of amusements than Tombstone. Only last evening—which, by the way, was an extra quiet one—there were meetings of the firemen, the Odd Fellows, the city council, and the literary and debating society, together with a ball, a theater, a dancing school, and a couple of private parties, all in full blast. Hurrah for Tombstone!

The most popular theaters managed to attract a broad section of the population with shows that would keep frontier audiences coming back for more. Tombstone became home to one of the most famous of these, the lively Bird Cage. In mid-January 1886, Joe Bignon and his wife Minnie purchased the then-defunct Bird Cage Theatre and reopened it as the Elite Theatre. To make his Elite Theatre a success, Mr. Bignon secured the services of several variety acts and maintained a good "stock" company. He also offered new faces weekly, dramatic performances, and a regular vaudeville show.

Bignon became an expert at appealing to the best and worst of his patrons. Not long after re-opening, the theater capitalized on the anti-Chinese movement that had swept through Tombstone. Taking advantage of the Chinese situation, the Elite offered a nightly play entitled *The Chinese Must Go!!* He placed a burlesque, or caricature, on his boards advertising the new play, and audiences packed the house.

Claret Sangaree

1½ ounces claret
1 teaspoon powdered sugar
1 tablespoon brandy

Shake the claret and sugar well with cracked ice, and strain into a 3-ounce cocktail glass. Be sure to leave enough room in the glass to float the brandy on top.

The play, based on the current situation in Tombstone, ended with a Chinaman being put on a burro with all his laundry implements, and being ridden out of town. While most enjoyed this version of the play, those who attended the final night's performance were treated to a different ending. The Chinaman was put on the burro with his things, but this time the burro refused to be led off the stage. Despite all efforts he stayed put. The *Daily Tombstone* wrote of the incident, "The situation was ludicrous in the extreme. His burroship had evidently joined the Pro-Chinese crowd; so far as he was concerned the almond-eyed disciples of Confucius could stay." Needless to say, the audience was so taken with the unexpected improvisation that laughter and cat-calls resonated throughout the theater.

Besides the usual performances and plays, Bignon brought in circus professionals, Mr. and Mrs. Taylor Frusch, to perform trapeze acts. After their indoor performances ended, the Fruschs set up a tent on a vacant lot on Allen Street and provided a grand outdoor performance. According to newspaper accounts, the Elite's next performances included Miss Eva St. Clair, the dashing serio-comic, and Little Bessie West, aged six, who danced and sang. Others on the playbill included Miss Maud Courtney and Miss Lulu Roze, both songbirds. Charles Keene, assisted by John West, William Hickey, and George Parker, handled the comedy.

The Elite offered something a little different in early May 1886 when it set up a walking-match racetrack around the audience. John McGarvin and John Forseek

---

Stone Fence
(Use a whiskey glass)

Cider
1 jigger of whiskey
2 or 3 lumps crushed ice

Fill the glass with cider [club soda can be substituted], stir up well, and serve; as a rule it is left for the customer to help himself to the whiskey if he so desires.

✦ AN IMMIGRANT'S IMPRESSIONS ✦

Andre Jorgenson Anderson was a native of Norway who settled in Texas in 1874. During an interview in the 1930s, Anderson recalled the range of establishments that greeted visitors in the up and coming town of Fort Worth: "The White Elephant was the most magnificent place in Ft. Worth in those days. It was located between Third and Fourth Streets on Main. It was a saloon, gambling house, and restaurant. There were no queens connected with the White Elephant. Before its opening, the place was advertised to be one of the finest combination saloons, gambling houses, and restaurants, without any exceptions. Those days ladies did not frequent saloons, but the good ladies of Fort Worth could not resist taking a look at the White Elephant during its opening night, and a large number came to look at the place.

"Upon entering the White Elephant, the people saw a filigree mahogany wood bar and back bar. All the glassware was cut glass of the highest grade and stacked high on the back bar. There was a large display of imported and domestic wines, liquors and cordials. The bartenders were dressed immaculately in white jackets, shirts, collars, and bow ties. Leading from the barroom was a wide stairway running to the second floor where the gambling room was located. On this stairway was laid the very best of carpet. At the entrance to the gambling room was a medium size table on which was stacked gold and silver coins, standing about six inches high. A uniformed man stood guard at this table. The men selected to run the various gambling games were chosen for their good looks as well as ability to operate a game. The excellent appearance of these men was the general talk among the ladies. Every game operator was dressed in a suit custom-made from the highest grade of cloth. They wore white stiff-front shirts with a conspicuous diamond stud in the bosom, a conspicuous diamond ring on the finger; and the charm, which hung from their watch chains, also contained a diamond. Those men were groomed in the latest of the day .... There was no charge for drinks to the patrons of the gambling room, and there were no restrictions on the kind of drinks served. The rule was to let the patrons drink and be merry, because the devices controlling the gaming tables took care of the proprietors. In addition, the more the patrons drank the more reckless they became with their money. Therefore, the free drinks were a good investment.'

Anderson then went on to describe a place at the other end of the spectrum: "At the other end of the saloon grade was the First and Last Chance saloon. It was located on Front Street (now Lancaster) across from the old depot. This was the place the 'cinches' patronized. It was the kind of a place patronized by the fellow who felt at home where he could expectorate on the floor at will, where he could sit down on the floor or lie down in a corner, and if one became too drunk for locomotion there was a room where one was placed until sobered. This saloon had one large room used for placing the drunks. The room contained no furniture, and men just lay on the floor. I have seen this drunkard's room packed like sardines in a can."

competed for $100. Both men walked heel to toe, first walking to the left for an hour, and then reversing for another hour. The process continued for a full six hours, when Forseek was declared the winner after walking the first mile in nine minutes and beating McGarvin by one lap.

The citizens of Tombstone weren't the only ones to consider strange shenanigans a regular part of town entertainment. J. W. Hagerty, a citizen of Fort Worth, Texas, remembered a theater in his town during the late 1880s. "Geo. Holland's Theatre was one of the principal show places," he recalled. "The place occupied an entire block and provided entertainment ranging from a wild animal zoo to a girl show, and some of the girls were not any too tame." Vaudeville acts "sizzled," and the theater drew a huge crowd. "Holland's Theatre was the center of what we called 'Hell's Half Acre,'" Hagerty recalled, "and it was an appropriate name. If there was anything ever invented by man to attract the base instinct of the human, which was not put on at Holland's, it was an oversight on the part of the management."

Hell's Half Acre, Oklahoma Territory, 1893.

But wherever the town was located, whatever its primary business, the saloons, gambling halls, and bordellos offered similar temptations.

A town in Nebraska had one of the most unusual houses in the West. According to old-timer Fred C. Scarborough, Robbers Cave was located near the old town of Lancaster, Nebraska about 1879. "It was at one time supposed to be a headquarters for outlaws and criminals, who used this place as a hideout .... It is even connected up with Pawnee Indian Spirit Legends, though probably visited only by the medicine men and chiefs." The entrance to the cave was through the basement of an old dance hall and sporting house. It became notorious as a thieves' hangout, and so, Scarborough continued, "in 1863 the Anti Horse Thief Association burned it down." Referring probably to the vigilantes' Klanlike disguise, he added, "The fire was set by white caps."

Scarborough also recalled a legend involving a famous outlaw who frequented Robbers Cave: "Frank Rawlins, who drove a hack for the 'White Elephant' Livery Barn in Lincoln, used to drive a 'Mr. Howard' out here often. Some thought this 'Mr. Howard' was Jesse James! This may have been. When we cleaned the cave we found an old carving:

> *A thief and a coward*
> *Was Mr. Howard*
> *But he laid as Jesse James*
> *in his grave."*

In Virginia City, Nevada, just about anyone could make money and become successful. It offered a variety of saloons and dance halls, designed to appeal to different cultures. The Boston Saloon was owned by William A. G. Brown, who was of African descent. He opened in 1864 on North B Street, but only a year before had been working as a shoeshine boy. By 1866 Brown had moved his prospering saloon to the corner of D and Union Streets in the heart of the entertainment district. Like many saloons in the Old West, the Boston had its share of brawls. In 1866 the *Territorial Enterprise* reported that at the Boston Saloon:

> … which is the popular resort for many of the colored
> population, about eleven o'clock, Sunday evening, a party of
> them were sitting around a table indulging in a 'friendly game
> of poker,' each one having … a pistol in his lap, when suddenly,
> by accident or otherwise, one of the pistols—a Deringer —fell
> upon the floor and exploded, causing a general consternation
> and scatteration …. The ball of the pistol took effect in the leg
> of a white man called "Frenchy," who, it appears, was one of
> the party and the only white man in the saloon. It passed
> through the calf of the left leg, taking out a piece of the bone,
> but not breaking it. The surgical skill of Dr. McMeane was
> brought to bear in the case, and the man is getting along very
> well, although it will be an ugly wound for some time.

Chapter 2

Boozers
and Boozing

"**G**IMME A WHISKEY!"

That line has resonated through thousands of books and films about the Old West, and with good reason. It was certainly the beverage of choice for many, but there were other reasons for whiskey's popularity in the saloons.

Why whiskey? An import of early Scotch-Irish settlers in the region, it was cheap and easy to make from an abundant supply of grain. Also, saloons, especially those in more remote areas, relied on what was delivered to them. In most cases, that was whiskey—of some sort. Larger towns held drinkers of more sophisticated tastes, and barkeeps had to keep an inventory of more expensive and more elaborate liquors. Behind the bar of the better establishments, the resident mixologist kept cordials, bitters, and syrups to make his many concoctions. In addition, he would also have had a variety of wines, champagne, sherry, port, brandy, and glasses to match. Some of the most popular libations of the day included: absinthe, vermouth, crème de chocolate, Benedictine, Hennessey and Martell brandies, Kirschwasser, anisette, mint cordial, and crème de cacao. Other offerings might include Holland and Old Tom gins, St. Croix or Jamaican rum, blackberry brandy, applejack, and schnapps.

As keen observer Mark Twain traveled the West, he wrote, "Moralists and philosophers have adjudged those who throw temptation in the way of the erring, equally guilty with those who are thereby led into evil." One could certainly apply that philosophy to both bartender and patron when a person tipped one too many glasses of whiskey.

Saloon owners ordered liquor from a variety of places, often including agents in California. One such company was Moore, Hunt & Co. in San Francisco. When ordering their stock, saloon owners chose from AA, A, B, or C brands. They also received discounts when they ordered in large quantities, such as cases or barrels. In the 1880s,

---

❖ AMARILLO NIGHTS ❖

Many saloons were so used to heavy drinkers that they developed special enclosures to deal with the casualties of an evening's revelry. Richard Murphy remembered the nights in Amarillo: "Some of the boys played the gambling joints, some just soaked themselves in the 'pizen,' and some went sally-hooting in the sally joints. Any kind of a joint that a fellow wanted was in the town to satisfy the waddies' wants. Nearly all the saloons in Amarillo, at that time, had bull-pens at the rear of the joints. The purpose for which the bull-pens were built was to have a place to shunt the fellows who became overloaded where they could sleep off the load of 'pizen'; also, to prevent interference from the law, or meddling gentry who were looking for a chance to swipe a roll of money. The bull-pen was also used for a battle ground. When a couple of fellows got riled at each other, they were shunted into the bull-pen to cool off. The saloon bouncers would take the guns away from the riled men and push them into the bull-pen to settle the argument, bear-fight fashion. That method saved a lot of shooting, but could not be worked in all cases and there was an occasional shooting. When I think of the Amarillo of those days, I recall a big sign that one saloon had in front of its place of business. It read: 'Whiskey, the road to ruin. Come in.'"

Evidence of excess after a night on the town.

Moore, Hunt & Co. was a main distributor of Kentucky whiskey to many Western towns. They also sold Anchor champagne, which cost $8.50 for five dozen pints, and Crown whiskey for $8 for a case. A barrel or half-barrel of AA brand whiskey cost $4 per gallon, while the same amount of C brand cost only $3. Some popular brands of U.S. whiskey included Thistle Dew, Old Crow, Hermitage, Old Kentucky, Old Reserve, Coronet, Log Cabin No. 1, O.K. Cutter, Chicken Cock and Rye, and Old Forrester. Imports included Dewar's Scotch, Jameson Irish Whiskey, and Canadian Club Whiskey.

In addition to liquor, many a schooner of beer was poured in saloons throughout the West, and creating a really good brew took great skill and know-how. Men who hailed from countries such as Germany and Switzerland, where beer-making is an art, started many breweries in the Old West.

After choosing the all-important hops and malt, the brewer's first task was to clean and grind the malt. Next was the process of "mashing," which entailed infusing the malt with water at a proper temperature to extract saccharine matter from the malt and change the starch into grape-sugar. The extract of malt was then drained into giant boilers to brew. After the brewing process was finished, the cooling began. The hot beer was pumped through large pipes to an immense flat tank where the beer was spread out. Once the beer was sufficiently cooled, the fermentation step took place. Yeast was added to the beer at a rate of one quarter of a pound to a pound and a half per barrel. After the beer had fermented, it was pumped into barrels to age. The next phase was called "racking," the process of drawing off the clear beer from the lees by pumping it out, leaving the dregs behind. Beer was generally stored for four to six months, and after aging sufficiently, was drawn off, or bottled.

Once made, the beer began its voyage to countless saloons throughout the West, some of them accessible only by stage or mule. Beer transport was occasionally dangerous. Henry Hollenstein, of Miller's Canyon, about thirty miles from Tombstone, was making a trip from the town to the railroad depot when tragedy struck. As he was driving his wagonload of empty kegs along a dirt road, the rope he used to tie the kegs broke. The kegs pushed Hollenstein to the ground and nearly crushed him to death. He lay unconscious for several hours before he was found and taken to the hospital.

More often, though, beer proved dangerous only after it went down the gullets of thirsty drinkers. William

---

Egg Nog
(Use a large bar glass)

Rich milk
1 fresh egg
¾ tablespoon sugar
⅓ glass of ice
1 small jigger of white rum
1 jigger of brandy

Fill the glass with rich milk [half-and-half will work well]; shake or stir ... the ingredients well together, and strain into a large bar glass; grate a little nutmeg on top, and serve. It is proper for the bartender to ask the customer what flavor he prefers, whether St. Croix or Jamaica rum. It is wise to be careful not to put too much ice into your mixing goblet, as by straining you might not be able to fill the glass properly, as it ought to be.

(Billy) Blevins, a former Texas Ranger, witnessed some of the first beer to travel to the new town of Toyah. "I remember the first keg of beer from Dallas that arrived out there. It was an introductory half-barrel keg. It was suggested by the foreman of an outfit with headquarters five miles from there that we have a barbecue on his ranch with all invited. We were to furnish the beer and the cowhands the meat."

Blevins recalled that beer in those days packed a little more punch than your average can of Budweiser: "That was some beer. The first glass caused one to see things and the next to hear things and with the third glass every person that talked to you would insult you. There were a good crowd from Toyah and cowhands from other outfits. Among the town folks was Jim Massey, a good friend of mine. We all ate barbecue and drank beer for a good spell. The crowd first became noisy, then quarrelsome and trying to keep the boys apart and from drawing their guns. Then suddenly Massey and I were shooting at each other and the rest of the crowd was trying to part us. Neither of us came close. Every time I shot I could see several Masseys and always picked the wrong one. It was the same with him he told me afterwards. That shooting exhibition ended the barbecue. The boys loaded the town gang in wagons and hauled us back to town. That gave the Dallas beer a good reputation, and it had the leading sale thereafter."

Cowhands were not the only ones to enjoy barley and hops. One Nebraska pioneer, Mrs. Lucie Belle Bartlett, recalled her childhood in Clay County. "Women very seldom came in saloons in those days, but would come to the back door for a bucket of beer. They called this 'Rushing the Growler.'" To believe ads in the *Daily Tombstone*, Geronimo would write to two of the city's beer vendors and express his preference for a cold brew. On November 17, 1885, an ad read:

SIERRA MADRES. AUGUST 27, 1885. Messrs. Caesar and Wehrfritz: see by late copies of the *Tombstone* that I was reported seriously wounded and it was thought I would die.

These reports are not correct, as I am not wounded nor am I dead, but I tell you that I am awful dry, and I want you to send me a consignment of that ice cold Anheuser beer that you are selling to the people of Tombstone. I only wish I was there to have it drawn from that German patent fountain. Geronimo.

The business partners Geronimo mentioned, Wehfritz and Caesar, owned the Crystal Palace Saloon and had certainly earned his patronage. In 1885, they constructed a patent refrigerator for storing beer, standing sixteen feet high and divided by an iron floor into two compartments. The lower part, for the beer, was six feet tall and held over a carload of kegs. The space above was large enough to hold a couple of carloads of ice. Within three or four days of its completion, residents were enjoying ice-cold beer direct from St. Louis breweries. The name of St. Louis proved effective for at least one other Tombstone beer seller as well. Business clearly went up at the St. Louis beer hall on Allen Street as pedestrians watched a mound in front of the saloon grow to more than eight hundred empty Gambrinus kegs that same year.

While beer was sometimes made locally, other U.S.-made beer was also distributed throughout the West. Popular beers of the time included Budweiser, Gambrinus, Fredericksburg, and Rebstock's St. Louis.

Early California winemakers also found a market in the Western saloon. Bottles of Sonoma wines could be had for 50 cents, half-bottles for 25 cents, and about 80 cents got you a gallon. California port, sherry, Angelica wine, and brandy were available as well. Swiss, Limburger, and American cheeses were also available. One wine-making company began its business in 1863, when it started producing sparkling wines. *Harper's Weekly* wrote, "The Buena Vista Company have pursued this enterprise with great success since 1863."

In July 1883, the *Tombstone Republican* carried a report on California wine. It appears they were taking an infestation in French

Early California winemaking.

vineyards as an opportunity to promote California wine consumption. Meanwhile, the *Pall Mall Gazette* reported:

> Now that the phylloxera has damaged beyond repair a large
> proportion of the vineyards in France, and the wine
> exporters have been obliged to supplement the natural grape
> juice with some less pleasant decorations, it might be well
> for some enterprising firm of wine merchants in England to
> turn their attention to the wines of California. In America,

the consumption of these wines is assuming larger
dimensions every year, and the Britisher in the New World
who allows strength of his prejudices is obliged to confess
the partiality of his hosts for the hocks and sauternes, the
ports and tokays, of their own country, is not misplaced.
There is one peculiarity about the cultivation of the wine in
California, which the vineyard owner of France and the hop
grower of England will learn with envy. For the last thirty
years there has not been a single season in which the crop
has not been a complete success.

Absinthe was another drink of choice for Victorians in the West.
Especially popular among the artists and writers of the nineteenth century, absinthe contains the ingredient wormwood (*Artemisia absinthi-
um*). Because it is so bitter, the liqueur needed sweetening to be palatable. As sugar does not readily mix with alcohol, the absinthe ritual
was born. A sugar cube was placed on a slotted spoon over the glass
containing a shot of clear peridot-green absinthe. When icy water was
drizzled through the sugar to melt it, the clear liqueur becomes cloudy
and palest jade in color. This signals that it is ready to drink.

Classic absinthe made with wormwood was banned for sale in
the U.S. in 1915 as part of a general temperance crackdown on all
intoxicating beverages. Wormwood was thought to cause hallucina-
tions and is still prohibited as a food additive by the FDA. The active
ingredient in wormwood is thujone, which is chemically similar to the
THC found in marijuana. It is important to note, however, that the
DEA has never designated absinthe as a controlled substance, and
wormwood is not classified as a drug.

Soda was another popular beverage in the West, and it was used
to make a variety of mixed drinks. In Tombstone, Frederick Blush
bought the Union Soda Works, at the corner of Second and Toughnut,
from Valentine Mand on July 19, 1881, for $900. Included in the sale

were the goods needed to run a soda manufacturing business and all the apparatus needed for making soda water, along with a horse and spring wagon.

Fort Worth had its own soda man in town by the late 1800s. Pioneer Bud Brown recalled, "My father, after his arrival here, considered the nature of business to enter for a livelihood. He chose the saloon business because it was one of the leading lines and doing the greatest business of all other lines during that period. He established a saloon at Third & Main Sts. and named it the 'Ruby Bar.' I recall the soda-water man of those days, because soda-water was my drink."

Drinking soda instead of whiskey proved dangerous for one Waco, Texas, resident. Charles Weibush told this story in the 1930s: "Until I was 16 years old I punched cattle about three months every spring and helped with the round-ups, branding the calves & dogies (which in the song of the dogies means when a little calf is left an orphan). When we had the round-ups, the cowboys would ride around the herd at night and sing the cowboy songs, sometimes just

---

Tom and Jerry

1 egg, separated
Powdered sugar
Pinch of baking soda
Hot milk
1 jigger of rum
½ ounce California brandy
Nutmeg

Beat the egg yolk in one bowl, and the white in another. Once they have been beaten separately, combine them together, and add enough powdered sugar to make a stiff batter. Add the baking soda and rum, stirring gently. Add a little more sugar to stiffen the batter again.

Dissolve 1 tablespoon of the batter in 3 tablespoons of hot milk, and place in a hot mug. Add the rum, and fill the mug with enough hot milk to come up ¼ inch from the top. Top with brandy and a grating of nutmeg.

Beef Tea

(All the rage in the late 1880s; use a hot-water glass or mug)

¼ teaspoon beef stock

Add the beef stock to the glass and fill with hot water. Mix with a spoon and hand it to the customer. Place pepper, salt, and celery salt near the customer in case they require it. Add a small amount of sherry wine or brandy, for which there should be no extra charge.

croon them to keep the herd quiet. The thoughts of the beautiful moonlight nights, the big herds and the cowboys, and the cool fresh air as the morning dawned gives me a homesick longing for the days of the range that nothing can fill the place. After the Houston and Texas Central railroad was built through to Waco, we often drove our cattle down to Marlin to load on the train to ship to Houston. I remember once when we went into a saloon and the boys took their drink, as I was so young they gave me soda water. (I was considered entirely too young to be allowed a drink of whiskey.) Soon some cowboys from another ranch came in and had their drinks, and one of them saw me and insisted that I have a drink of whiskey with him.

"When I refused, he took out his gun and began shooting at my feet and had me dance to keep out of the way of the bullets. To this I did my best, and pretty soon my crowd took it up and before they decided the question whether I was to dance or not to dance, there was a free-for-all fight, with no injury excepting a few swollen eyes and bumps from each other's fists. After they had settled this to their satisfaction they forgot me and called it a day."

The *Boise City Statesman* reported a similar incident in June 1881. The incident took place in Silver City, Idaho:

While George Palmer was standing at the counter of the Idaho Saloon, which adjoined the Idaho Hotel, Tim Warren came in and seized Palmer and jerked him around in a rough manner, but let go of him and said: "Come up and take a drink." Palmer declined, saying to Warren that he knew he never drank. Warren then started towards Palmer, when the latter slapped Warren in the face, and both went for their pistols. Palmer fired and hit Warren on the chin, but it glanced and only made a flesh wound. He, however, continued to fire, and the next ball went through Warren's right hand, in which he held his pistol, and the third shot ... lodged in Warren's shoulder, perfectly disabling him. There had been an old feud between the parties, and it is supposed that Warren took this opportunity to bring on a collision. There were several parties standing around and the bullets flew carelessly and caused a good deal of excitement.

Lemonade, cherryade, currantade, and orangeade were made by bartenders to help their customers beat the heat; some were made non-alcoholic, while others contained healthy doses of rum, wine, or brandy. "Temperance drinks" were also served in saloons for those "who had taken the pledge" or felt they had had too much. It was a mixologist's responsibility to know when his customer had too much to drink. Also available was a non-alcoholic ginger beer, ginger ale, sarsaparilla, and Apollonairis water.

A mixologist also stocked "mixers" that would have included mineral waters, soda water, carbonic acid, and cider. He also carried a variety of syrups: pineapple, strawberry, raspberry, lemon, and orange.

Managing and serving so many different forms of alcohol soon became a specialty all its own, and saloon owners employed skilled labor to serve them. In bigger towns, "mixologists" or bartenders of the time were highly skilled and prided themselves on their reputations. Sometimes these barkeepers were also jokingly referred to as pharmacists with a medicine chest. Local newspapers advertised when

This ad promotes whiskey as the Westerner's beverage of choice.

a new man was hired, and they listed the towns and bars in which he had previously served. The ads bragged that his previous skills were a guarantee that the establishment in question offered the best drinks in town. There were even books written in the late 1800s with instructions on how to set up a bar, what was proper and what was not, and how to make the drinks.

Harry Johnson tended bar in San Francisco and wrote the 1882 *Bartender's Manual,* which went into great detail as to how one should act and look behind the bar. It described how a bartender should address his customers, how he attained a job at a saloon and how to set up a bar, along with hints on making drinks just right. Harry stated that in order for a bartender to make the best drink possible, he must take the customer's order, and then ask if he liked it medium, stiff, or strong. He also needed to ascertain if the customer wanted a julep, a sour, or a toddy version of his drink. Harry concluded, "I cannot avoid, very well, offering more remarks regarding the conduct and appearance of the bartender .... Bartenders should not, as some have done, have a toothpick in their mouth, clean their finger nails while on duty, smoke, spit on the floor, or have other disgusting habits."

Even local papers observed and recognized mixologists of their time. *The Recorder*, a newspaper in San Francisco wrote:

Browsing in our favorite bookshop a familiar name caught the eye, Boothby! There it lay in its traditional paper covers of yellow and red, *Cocktail Bill Boothby's World Drinks and How To Mix Them*. A new edition, twice as thick as the last pre-prohibition issue, but breathing the flavor of alcohol and mint .... We knew Bill Boothby. Before coming to San Francisco he had mixed 'em and set 'em up "in the best houses" of New York, Chicago, Philadelphia, New Orleans, and Kansas City. He officiated behind the bar at Byron Hot Springs and was "presiding deity" (his own phrase) at the club house of Hotel Rafael in the gay days when Baron von Schroeder was making history over there. He was at the Silver Palace here. One edition of his book is dedicated "to the liquor dealers of San Francisco who unanimously assisted in my election to the Legislature by an unprecedented majority." Bill was in the Assembly in 1895, and there was no adverse liquor legislation that year, you may be sure. After that interruption to his real career, Bill was placed behind the famous bar of the Palace Hotel by the discriminating Colonel Kirkpatrick. They were all aces behind that mahogany, and Bill was the ace of aces. To see him rotating three cocktail glasses between the fingers of his left hand while measuring a jigger of gin or vermouth with the right was to witness a masterpiece of art in the making. Alas! Prohibition came, and Maxfield Parrish's "Pied Piper" looked down upon no more cocktail and highball devotees. Bill went to the Olympic Club to superintend a bar transformed to a soft drink counter. O, what a fall was there! It was the last position he held.

Jerry Thomas, considered to be the father of the cocktail, tended bar at the Occidental Hotel in San Francisco in the 1860s. One legend claims the martini's history starts at this hotel. As the story goes, a traveler on his way to Martinez, California, asked the hotel's mixologist to prepare something special—thus the martini (or Martinez) was created. The guest was not aware this barman was the legendary Professor Jerry Thomas, famous for his innovative cocktails. There are other stories of the martini's history, but there appears to be no actual proof of who really created it. In 1862, "Professor" Thomas played an important role in the history of the cocktail when he published his *Bartender's Companion*. He is also credited with creating the popular Tom and Jerry cocktail while tending bar at the Occidental.

Lemonade
(Use a large bar glass)

1½ tablespoon sugar
3 or 4 dashes lemon juice
¾ glass of shaved ice

Fill the balance with water; shake or stir well; dress with fruit in season, in a tasteful manner, and serve with a straw. To make this drink pleasant, it must be at all times strong; therefore take plenty of lemon juice and sugar.

Another story claims that in 1870 a gold miner stopped at Julio Richelieu's saloon in Martinez, California. The miner put a small pouch of gold and an empty bottle on the bar to be filled with whiskey. The miner wasn't happy with the trade, so Richelieu mixed up a small drink, plopped an olive in it, and named it after his town. Even now, Martinez, California, still claims to be the birthplace of the martini.

When did the name change from Martinez to martini? It appears it was around the late 1880s when the drink was so named by Harry Johnson in his book, *New and Improved Illustrated Bartender's Manual or How To Mix Drinks of the Present Style*, but Johnson's martini recipe was the same as everyone else's Martinez recipe. He may have possibly changed the name for other reasons. Harry's recipe book appears to be the first to spell the cocktail as "martini."

It took good instincts to separate drunken, armed Westerners from their hard-earned cash without initiating conflict.

The martini become steadily dryer as the nineteenth century came to a close. By 1891, William T. "Cocktail" Boothby's "Cocktail Boothby's American Bartender Martini" recipe omitted the sugar syrup, curaçao, and bitters, noting the sweetened gin and sweet vermouth "are both sweet enough." The critical step toward a true dry martini came in *Stuart's Fancy Drinks and How to Make Them*, by Thomas Stuart, which listed this 1896 martini variation as a "Marguerite": 1 dash orange bitters, 1 jigger dry gin, ½ jigger dry vermouth.

In addition to making good drinks, mixologists also had to learn how to handle their customers—it took good instincts to separate drunken, armed Westerners from their hard-earned cash without initiating a conflict. Tom J. Snow tended bar in Fort Worth during the 1880s, and he remembered many tense encounters. "At the time I worked as a bartender, Fort Worth was a pure cow town. Cowboys and ranchers, by the score, visited Fort Worth, bent on business and pleasure. My experience back of the bar, while waiting on the cowboys and ranchers, was interesting and enjoyable. For one to be successful as a dealer with the cowhands, it was necessary to take the fellows as they presented themselves. However, one could always depend on the cowmen playing fair."

Snow continued, "It wasn't just the high-born who enjoyed elaborate mixed drinks, however." He recalled cowboys who would ask for his priciest fare at any hour of the day. "One morning five waddies walked into the saloon and called for a 'frosty cocktail.' This particular drink was in great favor at the time and was among the expensive drinks. I mixed the five drinks and set the cocktails on the bar. The boys drank with great relish and commended me on my ability as a mixer of the cocktail."

Drinking and rough stuff usually didn't lead to fatalities, but it certainly made everyone aware of the strong presence of alcohol at every level of society. According to the *Tombstone Nugget*, different parts of the country had various sayings for being drunk and disorderly. In Gotham the drunk was "on a tear," in Chicago he was "on a hoorah," and in Kansas City he was "ginned up for all that's out." In Leadville "the galoot's on a roarer again," in Virginia City he was "on a toot," in Benson he was "pressing his tansy," and in Tombstone no one ever got drunk, although a fellow occasionally made "a holy show of himself."

Some were inspired to apply scientific reasoning to the widespread evidence of inebriation. Different varieties of alcohol proved an interesting subject for a man in San Francisco in the early 1880s. The man, whose identity is unknown, conducted a scientific study on Canal Street, where he studied intoxicated

---

Champagne Flip
(Use a large bar glass)

1 fresh egg
½ tablespoon sugar
½ glass shaved ice
1½ jiggers of Champagne

Shake it well until it is thoroughly mixed, strain it into a fancy bar glass, grate a little nutmeg on top, and serve. This is a very delicious drink, and it gives strength to delicate people.

✦ WILD WESTERN SYNONYMS ✦ FOR ALCOHOLIC DRINK

Agua ardiente	Irrigation	Salteur liquor
Awerdenty	Jag	Scamper juice
Base burner	Jig juice	Scorpion Bible
Benzine	Kansas sheep dip	Sheepherder's delight
Boilermaker and his helper	Lamp oil	Shinny
	Leopard sweat	Snake-head whiskey
Brave maker	Lightning	Snake poison
Brigham Young cocktail	Lightning flash	Stagger soup
	Mescal	Station drink
Bug juice	Mountain dew	Strong water
Bumblebee whiskey	Neck oil	Strychnine
Choc	Nose paint, nose varnish	Sudden death
Coffin varnish		Tanglefoot
Conversation fluid	"Oh to be joyful"	Tansy
Corn	Pair of overalls	Taos lightning
Cowboy cocktail	Pass brandy, Pass whiskey, etc.	Tarantula juice
Dehorn		Tequila
Drunk water	Pine top	*Tiswin*
Dust cutter	Pizen	Tonsil paint, tonsil varnish
Dynamite	Pop skull	
Educated thirst	Prairie dew	Tongue oil
Firewater	Red disturbance	Tornado juice
Fool's water	Redeye, hundred-yard redeye	Trade whiskey
Forty rod		Valley tan
Gut warmer	Red ink	White mule
Honeydew	Rookus juice	Wild mare's milk

men to determine what kind of alcohol they drank. A reporter approached the scientific man with a notebook and asked, "You are an artist perhaps?" "No, sir," said the man with the book. "My object is a scientific one. I am collecting facts designed to throw light upon the internal condition of the inebriate by noting his acts when intoxicated. Patients get too much of the lump treatment."

The Wicked West

The scientist went on to claim,

A gin drinker resisted the influence better after the first few drinks and became more helpless after he had his quantum, more than the majority of the drinkers of spirits. Gin drinkers, however, recovered easily, although they often got sick.... The whiskey drinker got lively and excited and was often hard-headed and obstinate. His gyrations were most eccentric of all. The bracing power of whiskey was followed by unpleasant cerebral activity ... it took hold of a man. Imbibers rarely fell down ... those who liked Irish whiskey took a sort of 'cow-path' route. Scotch whiskey connoisseurs developed an easy, rolling, liberal gait, and drinkers of this libation are subject to various peculiarities.

St. Croix rum drinkers did not talk loudly, nor sway as much as the whiskey drinker did. A rum drinker kept more clearheaded, but was prone to get weak in the knees. When they walked, they took a few straight steps, and they suddenly veered sidewise.

According to the scientist, all these theories were null and void if the consumer had mixed his choice of beverage. In applejack, the victim almost always fell upon his back. In walking, he raised his feet as if trying to climb stairs. Drinkers of applejack seemed to become intoxicated rather quickly—it acted as a sleeping aid and was more potent than rye whiskey. The scientist said of applejack, "Its power of raising the imagination to a high degree of foolishness is well known."

Chapter 3

For Medicinal Use Only?

W HAT WE THINK OF TODAY as over-the-counter drugs were also around in the Old West, but they were used, sold, and even prescribed without much government regulation. Alcohol was considered a cure-all, and many so-called "tonics" or "elixirs" were nothing more than good old whiskey in a brand-new bottle. One recipe for relieving rheumatism called for "half ounce of black cohosh root to one pint of best rye ...." Dr. Chase's 1880 recipe recommended one to three teaspoons three times per day just before meals.

Another of Dr. Chase's recipes included various tree barks, a half pound of prickly ash berries, and spikenard root. The "medicine" was put in a gallon jug that was then filled with brandy. This remedy was for chronic rheumatism, and the sufferer was advised to have three wine glasses of this mixture daily. Other remedies called for wine, Jamaican rum, gin, morphine, opium, and laudanum.

No one really knows just how much "rheumatiz" Western pioneers actually suffered, but we do know that cures for such ailments were intoxicatingly widespread. Some claimed they were visiting the "professor" at their favorite saloon to be cured of something—or at least drown their pain in a tasty medicinal treatment!

Simmond's Kentucky Nabob Pure Bourbon Whiskey was a popular elixir in the 1880s. The ads read:

The Wicked West

Medical Journals say that Simmond's Nabob Whiskey is a safe stimulant and very wholesome; can be safely used by all invalids; all who value their health should use Simmond's Nabob Whiskey; it is the purest and the best in the Market; being analyzed by the most eminent professors and pronounced by them free from any adulteration, and recommended for medicinal and family use .... It has a very fine flavor and is mild from old age; give it a trial, you then can judge for yourselves; sold by barrels, half barrels, and cases by my agents on liberal terms. Endorsed by all leading physicians; kept by all druggists, grocers, and first-class saloons. Beware of counterfeits; none genuine unless labeled with the signature and brand on the bottle.

While many believe that opium came to the American West with the Chinese immigrants, the history of opium and its close cousins, laudanum and morphine, was much older and far more commonplace than most realize. John Jacob Astor built a significant portion of his fortune in the opium trade, and as early as the 1850s, many had begun to recognize addiction to opium and related drugs as a significant social problem.

It's easy to understand why so many people in the West became addicted to these drugs. Many "prescriptions" or "recipes" either included or called for these drugs straight. Oftentimes conditions in the West were tough: miners were injured, cowhands were hurt, and there were saloon fights. Opium and laudanum were standard remedies for milder problems, while morphine handled the tough stuff. Opium was used to cure colds, fevers, pleurisy, and inflammation of the lungs. Laudanum was used for headaches, toothaches, neuralgia, sore eyes, and in cough syrup. Morphine was used in cough lozenges, but also administered straight for surgery and gunshot patients.

By 1874, San Francisco had banned opium smoking within the city limits, confining the practice to Chinatown's opium dens, and back in Virginia City Mark Twain penned, "What the Chinese quarter of Virginia was like—or, indeed, what the Chinese quarter of any Pacific coast town was and is like—may be gathered from this item, which I printed in the *Enterprise* while reporting for that paper:

Patent medicine vendors did a lively business in days when liquor was plentiful and doctors scarce.

CHINATOWN. - Accompanied by a fellow reporter, we made a trip through our Chinese quarter the other night. The Chinese have built their portion of the city to suit themselves; and as they keep neither carriages nor wagons, their streets are not wide enough, as a general thing, to admit of the passage of vehicles. At ten o'clock at night the Chinaman may be seen in all his glory. In every little cooped-up, dingy cavern of a hut, faint with the odor of burning Josh-lights and with nothing to see the gloom by save the sickly, guttering tallow candle, were two or three yellow, long-tailed vagabonds, coiled up on a sort of short truckle-bed, smoking opium, motionless and with their lusterless eyes turned inward from excess of satisfaction—or rather the recent smoker looks thus, immediately after having passed the pipe to his neighbor—for opium-smoking is a comfortless operation, and requires constant attention. A lamp sits on the bed, the length of the long pipe-stem from the smoker's mouth; he puts a pellet of opium on the end of a wire, sets it on fire, and plasters it into the pipe much as a Christian would fill a hole with putty; then he applies the bowl to the lamp and proceeds to smoke—and the stewing and frying of the drug and the gurgling of the juices in the stem would well-nigh turn the stomach of a statue. John likes it, though; it soothes him; he takes about two dozen whiffs and then rolls over to dream, Heaven only knows what, for we could not imagine by looking at the soggy creature. Possibly in his visions he travels far away from the gross world and his regular washing and feasts on succulent rats and birds' nests in Paradise.

Many Western towns had a Chinese quarter or section. Men frequented the opium dens, but the fact was that women and children frequented them as well. In April 1877, the *Territorial Enterprise* reported on police action against the drug: "Officers ... made a successful raid on one of the opium-smoking dens in Chinatown and captured four young men and a girl, all American. They were at 3 p.m. taken before Judge Knox, tried (with a single exception) and found guilty of being inmates of one of those damnable places .... There they sat, with eyes lusterless and bleared and fixed on vacancy, in a dreamy, semi-unconscious state, more terrible than death itself."

The problem of opium addiction in turn gave rise to increased suspicion of those who were popularly blamed for purveying the "yellow peril"—or the Chinese immigrants as well as those who continuously smuggled drugs into the country. The *San Francisco Morning Call* printed this opium story on July 9, 1864:

The ingenuity of the Chinese is beyond calculation. It is asserted that they have no words or expressions signifying abstract right or wrong. They appreciate "good" and "bad,"

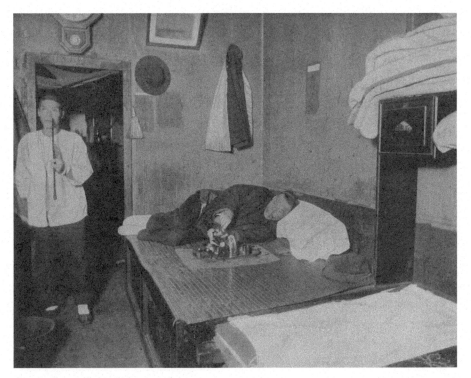

A rare photo of a typical opium den.

but it is only in reference to business, to finance, to trade, etc. Whatever is successful is good; whatever fails is bad. So they are not conscience-bound in planning and perfecting ingenious contrivances for avoiding the tariff on opium, which is pretty heavy. The attempted swindles appear to have been mostly, or altogether, attempted by the Coolie passengers—the Chinese merchants, either from honorable motives or from policy, having dealt honestly with the government. But the passengers have reached the brains of rascality itself, to find means for importing their delicious drug without paying the duties. To do this has called into action the inventive genius of brains equal in this respect to any that ever lodged on the top end of humanity. They have, doubtless, for years smuggled opium into this port continuously. The officers of customs at length got on their track, and the traffic has become unprofitable to the Coolies, however well it has been paying the officials through the seizures made. The opium has been found concealed in double jars and brass eggs, as heretofore described, brought ashore in bands around the body, and by various other modes. The latest dodge detected was sausages, bolognas, as it were, filled with opium; and yesterday we saw a tin can, with a false bottom about one third the distance from the base ....

Newspapers and periodicals began to recognize the fact that people had drug problems. In *Harper's Weekly*, August 1885, an ad for a product appeared with the title, "Opium Habit Cured Quickly." They advertised that the problem could be cured "secretly" and "quietly" in the privacy of one's own home without pain, nervousness, or loss of sleep.

Increased awareness, not to mention the staggering increase in drug addicts, led to the earliest regulation of narcotics by Congress in 1890 and a widely publicized campaign against the "Yellow Peril."

Laudanum was a widely used ingredient in

Too often, prostitutes were prisoners of both their employers and opium.

many medications as well as used alone. An opium product, which consisted basically of opium dissolved in alcohol, laudanum was regularly recommended for anything from mild headaches to toothache, and was particularly favored for "female troubles." Unfortunately, it was also highly addictive.

The following letter penned by an anonymous woman and entitled "Confessions of a Young Lady Laudanum-Drinker" appeared in *The Journal of Mental Sciences,* January 1889:

Dear Sir,

Perhaps you may remember a lady calling on you with her daughter about the middle of August, to ask you if there was any way of curing the habit of taking opium, which the girl had contracted. I, who write, am that same girl, and think you may perhaps be interested to hear how I got on. It is hateful to me to think of that horrible time, and one of my chief reasons for writing to you is to beg you to try and make known by every means in your power, what a terrible thing opium-eating is. If people only knew of the consequences sure to follow on such a habit, of its insidiousness, and the difficulty of leaving it off, surely they would never touch it.

Perhaps it is rather soon for me to imagine myself cured, but I do not think I can ever feel more horrified about it than I do now. There was no excuse for me taking it, brought up by such a mother, and with such a constant example of unselfishness before me in the rest of the family. All my tastes and fancies were gratified; as mother says, when I take a whim into my head, the whole house is turned upside down. When I came home from school I insisted on practicing seven hours a day, and the family put up with it, though it was a great infliction to them. It would have been better for me had they not done so, for I was naturally so tired-out at night that I could not sleep, and knowing that sleep would come easily with a little laudanum, it was difficult to resist taking it.

Of course, it didn't become habitual all at once; the first time I got it was at school, after a concert, when its effects were so soothing that it became quite usual for me to get it, mixed up with quinine .... None but those who have as completely succumbed to it as I did could guess the mischief it would do. Even you, with an experience which must be extremely varied, being as you are in such a good place for studying people's brains (or rather their want of them), cannot know the amount of harm it did to me morally, though I must say you did seem to have a pretty fair idea of it. It got me into such a state of indifference that I no longer took the least interest in anything and did nothing all day but loll on the sofa reading novels, falling asleep every now and then, and drinking tea. Occasionally I would take a walk or drive, but not often. Even my music I no longer took much interest in, and I would play only when the mood seized me, but felt it too much of a bother to practice .... Worse than all, I got so deceitful that no one could tell when I was speaking the truth. It was only this last year it was discovered ... and it was my married sisters who first began to wonder what had come over me. They said I always seemed to be in a half-dazed state and not to know what I was doing .... By that time it was a matter of supreme indifference to me what they thought, and even when it was found out, I had become so callous that I didn't feel the least shame. Even mother's grief did not affect me, I only felt irritated at her; this is an awful confession to have to make, but it is better to tell the whole truth when you once begin, and it might be some guide to you in dealing with others. If you know of anyone indulging in such a habit, especially girls, just tell them what they will come to.

Of course its effects differ according to one's nature, and it's to be hoped few get so morally degraded as I did. This much is certain, few would have the constitution to stand it as I did, and even I was beginning to be the worse for it. For one thing, my memory was getting dreadful; often, in talking to people I knew intimately, I would forget their names and make other absurd mistakes of a similar kind. As my elder sister was away from home, I took a turn at being house-keeper. Mother thinks every girl should know how to manage a house, and she lets each of us do it in our own way, without interfering. Her patience was sorely tried with my way of doing it, as you may imagine; I was constantly losing the keys, or forgetting where I had left them. I forgot to put sugar in puddings, left things to burn, and a hundred other things of the same kind.

One thing I would like to know, and that is—whether you could tell that I had not left off laudanum that day we called. Surely you must know the state one gets into when suddenly deprived of it; they could no more sit up and speak as I did than fly. By that time I had brought myself down to a quarter of an ounce a day, and as you had put mother on her guard, I had no means of getting any more. (I hate having to own that I tried to do so.) So the day after we saw you was the last I had any. Then began a time I shudder to look back upon. I don't like owning to bodily suffering, but will not deny that I suffered then. I wonder if leaving off opium has the same effect on everyone! My principal feeling was one of awful weariness and numbness at the end of my back; it kept me tossing about all day and night long. It was impossible to lie in one position for more than a minute, and of course sleep was out of the question. I was so irritable that no one cared to come near me; mother slept on the sofa in my room, and I nearly kicked her once for suggesting that I should say hymns over to myself, to try and make me go to sleep. Hymns of a very different sort were in my mind; I was once or twice very nearly strangling myself; and I am ashamed to say that the only thing that kept me from doing so was the thought that I would be able to get laudanum somehow. I was conscious of feeling nothing but the mere sense of being alive, and if the house had been burning, would have thought it too much of an effort to rise ....

It wasn't long before most Americans began to realize the country had a drug problem and ads for various "cures" appeared.

However, I gradually got over that, and I now am perfectly well, with the exception of my back, which has that nasty aching feeling now and then. Our medical man, who is a bright specimen of the country doctor, said "it might be anything," and when asked to explain what that meant said, "perhaps her corsets are too tight."

Oh, why do you doctors not try prevention as well as cure? You have it in your power to warn those who take laudanum now and then for toothache or headache what an insidious thing it is and how easily they may become the victims of it. I began that way, and see what it came to? You doctors know all the harm those drugs do, as well as the "victims" of them, and yet you do precious little to prevent it. If that subject were to be taken up instead of some so often spoken of in the health lectures which are now given, it might do some practical good. Well, I wonder at myself being able to write such a long letter on a subject which is so repugnant to me that I try never even to think of it. I can hardly finish up in my usual style which is "hoping to see you soon again," because I certainly don't hope so, and if I ever do have the pleasure of seeing you again, let us hope it will be under very different circumstances.

Morphine, invented in 1805, was first celebrated as a cure-all. It was thought that morphine "tamed" opium, and it was ironically used in the treatment of many opium addicts. In fact, morphine proved to be a highly dangerous, addictive drug that destroyed many lives in the Old West. Research reveals another historical irony in that the number of female morphine addicts far outnumbered male addicts by as many as two thirds. Like its "sister" drug, laudanum, morphine was widely and irresponsibly prescribed by many physicians for the treatment of "female troubles." In addition, consumption of alcohol by women was often frowned upon, while the taking of morphine and laudanum, especially under a doctor's advice, was within the bounds of respectable behavior—until, of course, it got out of hand.

Mrs. Erret Hicks of Canyon City, Oregon remembered a story associated with the fire of 1898: "The evening of the fire an out-of-town minstrel troupe was playing at

> **Morphine, invented in 1805, was first celebrated as a cure-all.**

the local opera house. The last song of the evening was a solo called 'There Will Be A Hot Time in the Old Town Tonight.' After the performance everyone returned to their homes. In a short while the fire bell rang out the fateful news. The old hotel was on fire. All that night the townspeople fought the fire. Our home was turned into a community kitchen. We cooked ham, eggs, toast, and coffee until I thought I could never face an egg again as long as I lived. Oh yes, and hot biscuits by the hundreds we made. One reason was because it was colder than Greenland's icy mountains, despite the heat from the flames. Well, the story about the fire is that the fellow that sung the song was a morphine addict. To make the song a real hit, he burned the town down. At least we know that he disappeared during the night and was never heard from again."

During her 1939 interview she remembered when some men were digging up a main in the town. At that time they found a boot, and some man laughed and said, "I guess it belongs to ————." The name escaped her memory, but the reference was made to the man who burned the town.

Chapter 4

Up in Smoke

WHEREVER ALCOHOL WENT IN THE OLD WEST, it seemed that tobacco followed right behind. They were usually enjoyed together in most saloons and dance houses, though regular smokers might purchase cigarettes, tobacco, and cigars just about anywhere. Saloons, gambling halls, stationary stores, and mercantile stores all featured tobacco products. Some advertised "Genuine Durham, Seal of North Carolina, Old Judge, and Vanity Fair Tobacco." Others advertised "Smoke Gauymede cigars, 2 for 25 cents," and "Chew Out of the Sea tobacco." Cigar varieties were endless and included Key West, Owl, Club House, Española, Plantation, and Hespero brands. Many saloon owners received consignments of cigars from  San Francisco, which were offered in a box from $3.50 to $13 per hundred.

Soon after she was married in 1875, Pauline Meyer traveled from her home in San Francisco to join her husband in New Mexico. After a journey of about two weeks, she reached her new home in a little Mexican settlement about twenty-five miles southwest of

THE BEST IN THE MARKET.

Albuquerque in Bernalillo County. Mr. Meyer had a general merchandise store there. He sold the natives sugar and coffee and yards of calico for shirts and dresses, shoes, nails, and kerosene oil. When Mr. Meyer was away buying sheep, Mrs. Meyer had to tend the store. At first she couldn't understand a thing the people said to her, but she very soon learned the names of most of the articles in the store and how to use the simple greetings *buenos días* and *como le va!* Even after she was able to speak the language fairly easily, their brown faces seemed strange to her. "I suppose it would be right in style now," she said, "but in those days I thought I'd never seen anything like those women sitting around the store with cigarettes in their mouths, always laughing and happy."

The *Denver Republican* printed a story on November 15, 1897, entitled "Cigarette License Law":

> The city License Department is engaged in gathering statistics of the sellers of cigarettes in the city. It is estimated that there are about 600 cigarette dealers. It is not the intention of the department to enforce the anti-cigarette

ordinance against each of the dealers. The policy will be to select a few of the larger ones, summon them to the police court, and allow Police Magistrate Ellis to pass upon the legality of the measure .... One of the largest dealers in cigarettes in the city tendered the license fee of $1,000 Saturday to the License Department. The tender, however, was accompanied by a written protest, which it was requested should be filed with the fee. Inspector Vick Roy declined to accept the $1,000 unless the protest was withdrawn, but this was emphatically refused.

Even though smoking was generally accepted, and sometimes expected, some Tombstone city council members did not agree. In early February, while council was in session, member Flynn and clerk Chapin began smoking. The mayor immediately ordered them to quit. A motion was then made to suspend the rules so smoking could be allowed, but the motion was defeated. The mania to indulge overcame the gentlemen, and they began smoking again. Mr. Thomas again moved that the council be allowed to smoke during sessions. Mr. Dean seconded the motion, and a vote was taken; however, the result was the same. The vote was reconsidered and members Thomas and Dean voted "aye," Thomas Atchison voted "no," and Mr. Nash remained silent. The mayor voted "no" to the smoking motion, so quiet Alderman Nash was forced to vote and said "aye." Mr. Thomas asked that the motion

Even though smoking was generally accepted, and sometimes expected, some Tombstone city council members did not agree.

This interesting mix of symbols shows the "wisdom" of a good cigar.

not be put on the books, but Atchison strongly objected and argued, "that we make a smoking room of the city hall" be properly noted in the minutes. It was so ordered.

Tobacco, for one man and his friends, proved to be a life saver. W. H. Thomas of Graham, Texas, recalled a story from the 1890s. "Four of us punchers are coming out of a saloon in Graham along in the wee wee hours of the morning when a masked gunman sticks us up. Well, with that thing looking as big as a cannon to us, we 'put 'em up.' He tells us to pass our sixers to him, one at a time and with the butts toward him. Now, J. D. was rolling a Bull Durham when we come out of the saloon, and he still had the t'baccy in the paper in his hand and up over his head. When his hand gets even with his mouth on its way down to his scabbard, he blows the t'baccy in the gunman's eyes and jumps to one side. The gunman shoots but he can't see where he is shooting because the Bull Durham is burning him up. You try that sometime and see how it burns. Well, all four of us jump right on him and we're stomping him right into the boardwalk when the sheriff comes running up after hearing the shots. He takes the man to jail, but you know how those old time jails were. He got out that night and is still gone, but he's carrying a souvenir from that stomping."

Many a cigar was smoked during Tombstone's boom, so it was good news when George Walker's Key West cigar store advertised it could be found on Allen, between Fifth and Sixth Streets, in late July 1882. Walker stated he received a large invoice of the celebrated Stratton & Storm's Bouquet cigars, Key West brand, and the Grand Central cigar. He also carried a full line of smoker's supplies, including meerschaum and briar-wood pipes. Next door to the cigar store stood the Key West Saloon, owned by James Brophy, which offered

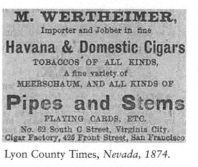

Lyon County Times, *Nevada, 1874.*

beer, wine, liquor, and cigars to wholesale and retail markets.

Cigar stands were extremely popular in saloons and dance halls. Like a gambling concession, the saloon owner often did not own it, but received a portion of the profits. If a saloon owner offered cigars, he offered customers more than just a drink. It was thought that if a saloon owner offered good quality cigars at a reasonable price, then his other business would come as well.

✦ TOBACCO TERMINOLOGY ✦

Bible—book of cigarette papers
Brain tablet—cigarette
Chaw—cut of plug tobacco for chewing
Cigarrito—small cigar
Dream book—cigarette papers
Fill a blanket—to roll a cigarette
Heifer dust—snuff
Hoja—cornhusk cigarette wrapper
Killickinnic, kinnikinnick—Indian herbal smoking mixture
Makin's—materials for making cigarettes
Paper-collar stiff—cigarette
Pimp stick—cigarette
Plew—pipe plug tobacco
Ponche—tobacco
Prayer book—book of cigarette papers
Punche—cheap tobacco
Quirly—cigarette
Rest powder—snuff
Rollin's—cigarette tobacco
Salve eater—snuff dipper
Scandihoovian dynamite—snuff (see snoose)
Shuck—cigarette paper
Seegar—cigar
Single Twist—brand of tobacco
Smoke—a cigarette; also a measure of time, based on the time it took
    to smoke one
Snoose, snooze—strong, moist Scandinavian snuff
Swedish condition powder—snuff (see snoose)

Then, as now, pretty girls made for good advertising.

In *Following the Equator*, Mark Twain wrote, "When I was a youth I used to take all kinds of pledges, and do my best to keep them, but I never could, because I didn't strike at the root of the habit—the desire; I generally broke down within the month. Once I tried limiting a habit. That worked tolerably well for a while. I pledged myself to smoke but one cigar a day. I kept the cigar waiting until bedtime, then I had a luxurious time with it. But desire persecuted me every day and all day long; so, within the week I found myself hunting for larger cigars than I had been used to smoke; then  larger ones still, and still larger ones. Within the fortnight I was getting cigars made for me—on a yet larger pattern. They still grew and grew in size. Within the month my cigar had grown to such proportions that I could have used it as a crutch. It now seemed to me that a one-cigar limit was no real protection to a person, so I knocked my pledge on the head and resumed my liberty."

Cigars weren't just for smoking during the late nineteenth century. They were also used to help cure ringworm. *Dr. Chase's 1880 Recipes* book advised, "Take the best Cuban cigars, smoke one sufficient length of time to accumulate one-fourth or one-half of ashes upon the end of the cigar." He then advised to rub the ashes into the area needing treatment three times daily.

Chapter 5

Let the Games Begin

A GAMBLING SPIRIT IS WHAT INSPIRED many people to head West in the first place. After working hard on a cattle drive or digging in a mine, men needed a way to relax and have fun. In keeping with that risk-taking spirit, many chose to wager their hard-earned money in the saloon. If any activity could compete with drinking for the title of most popular in the Old West, it would be gambling. To many of them, the wild swings of fortune at the poker table reflected the strange paths fate had led them down.

William "Billy" Mayer, a pioneer resident of Portland, Oregon, recalled just such a twist of fate: "Don't amount much to nothing. Just shows what a fool a fellow makes of himself getting drunk; in the early 1900s I was making pretty good money and I spent it, mostly on booze. Finally I decided to cut the liquor out. I sobered up and saved my money and put it in the bank. There was a bank—I don't remember its name— up on Sixth and Washington streets. I put my money in that. Kinda funny, we always associate snakes with drinking, and there was a snake that run up and down the sign on that bank; anyway it looked like a snake. Electricity running 'round letters was just being introduced. Well I put my money there till I got $200. I was feeling pretty good. Then one morning I went up to the bank to deposit $20, and it was closed. All my money gone to hell. The lid was off from that minute."

The Wicked West

Mayer continued, "I got good an' drunk an' before night I was dead-broke, the $20 gone an' all the loose change I had besides. I had a big gold watch that I'd carried a long time. All my friends knew it. It had a lighthouse engraved on the face of the lid. I was still pretty drunk, but I wanted to raise some dough, so I wandered up Third Street to a saloon where there was a friend of mine. I thought he'd lend me $10 on the watch. His saloon had a ladies' entrance, just like they all had them days. I went in the ladies' entrance, an' I was showin' this friend the watch, an' while we was talking about it, a girl came out one of the rooms. She saw the watch and said, 'Let me see it.' Not having my wits about me, I handed it over and just like a flash she was gone through the door. I dashed after her, but she'd gone through one door and I'd gone through another. She wasn't any place to be found, and she took my watch with her. I sure was broke then. Well, the funny part of the whole story is that a good while afterwards I was in a saloon … when in comes a fellow from the street. He had a watch, and he wanted to know what the saloonkeeper would give for it. The saloonkeeper was an old friend of mine, and right away he grabbed the watch. I paid $40 for it and got it back."

Frank G. Heiner of Montana also recalled how the old-timers spent their hard-earned money as soon as they made it. "We all had money, and we all blew it in as soon as we got it. I remember when I made fourteen dollars a day workin' in the drift, and I wouldn't have enough to pay my board bill at the end of the week. Expenses were high, but I lost most of it buckin' the tiger, that is, faro bank. The saloons were full all the time. There were shootin' scrapes every day, but that didn't make no difference in the population. There were always new people in town, cattlemen, miners, road agents."

Most towns had all sorts of betting tables in different establishments, most willing to accept anything from dollar bills to mine claims and gold dust as payment or ante. Fort Worth resident Andre Jorgenson Anderson remembered the dizzying array of betting

Casino chips were good as gold and sometimes better. (Chips courtesy of Tombstone Western Heritage Museum.)

options in his town. "Most establishments, whether big and fancy, or plain and small, usually sported some sort of gambling concession. Saloons offered a wide variety of games, including billiard tables, roulette wheels, and faro tables. The types of card games or banking games played in a saloon were as different as the patrons."

Twenty-one, faro, monte, 7-up, lansquenet, keno, and an endless variety of pokers were common in most saloons.

According to Texan F. Forsgard, codes of conduct surrounded gambling in the Old West. Forsgard was born there in 1870 and vividly recalled the gamblers of his childhood: "Lots of gambling went on. It was a regular business. There were several men who had saloons and gambling halls; usually the gambling places were in a room over

Working girls enjoy a game of billiards.

the saloon. These men were square-shooters, they had their families here and they were treated like any other respected citizens of the town. If they caught any of their dealers or any player cheating or playing a crooked game, they would tell him that he had to get out and would ask him where he wanted to go, and when he told them they would buy him a ticket there, put him on the stage, and see that he left town. They wouldn't allow any toughs to stay in town, or any cheap gamblers. If any came in, they would tell them to get out in twenty-four hours, and if he didn't, they ran him out."

Clara Brown, the journalist who described many of the major events in early Tombstone, described the bettors' scene for the *Californian* in July 1881:

> Liquor and gambling saloons are a conspicuous feature of
> the streets, both in point of numbers and elegance of finish.

Strains of music issue from these attractive rooms, drawing in the idle crowd; and fortunate is he who does no farther than to curiously scan the progress of the games. Some of those who participate therein, may leave with heavier pocket-books than were theirs when they went in, but the majority will depart with flat purses. It is an old saying that plenty of gambling is a sure indication of a prosperous camp. Professional gamblers will not remain long where no profits are to be made, and that plenty of money is in circulation is a pretty good sign of abundant-yielding mines. There were ten faro games, besides innumerable monte, keno, poker, and snap games.

One North Dakota town placed bets on something most other towns did not—corpses. Robert Lee Fuller recalled his life in the 1890s: "One of the [things] I did after I left Llano [Texas], was to go to Wildrose, North Dakota. That was a rough, frontier town that dealt with range hands and so on. I lit there in the wintertime when it was so-o cold. The day I got in, some cowhands had brought in some nesters that had froze in their cabin. They'd burnt their wood, then burnt their furniture. The cowpunchers found them froze stiff and still in bed. They just brought these nesters in just as-is. They was still stiff as a board when they got to Wildrose, so they took the stiffs to the saloon. The saloonkeeper sent a barsweep to the proper authorities, and had the cowpunchers lean the [stiffs] up against the wall. Do you know them stiffs leaned that way for two days, and the gamblers sat around, making bets on when they'd cave? They never did cave 'til the right people got there to handle it."

For some gamblers, their wealth stayed with them only for the trip from the mine to the saloon, without even a stop to convert ore into dollars. "Gambling was one of the chief diversions the men had after working all day," began Mrs. Neil Niven, speaking of life in Granite,

Oregon, during the late 1800s. "Of course, most of the things I know about that life is hearsay. I never went into a saloon in my life. It wasn't a thing a lady could do. I remember one time a miner had just made a big strike up the hill back of town. When he brought his bag of dust in he walked up to the saloon, and while standing at the door, he threw his bag of gold dust across the room and it lit on the bar, breaking the bag and making a big dent in the bar. He yelled at the top of his voice to everyone in the place, 'Come on, you mud sluckers, the drink is on me.' It was one of the wildest, wooliest nights that Granite ever had."

The notorious Poker Alice, who once said: "I'd rather deal than eat."

A gunfighter, gambling, and diamonds led to death in San Antonio, Texas, in 1884. On March 13, 1884, *The Daily Capitol* published an account of gunfighter and lawman Ben Thompson:

> The same reasons exist with regard to the difficulty between him and Jack Harris, in this same [Vaudeville] Theater at San Antonio, where Ben Thompson, Tuesday night, met his death. The incidents of the homicide and the subsequent trial and acquittal of Thompson are still fresh in the minds of people of both Austin and San Antonio. But these two tragedies are both an outgrowth of the same cause; it is deemed best to recapitulate the two homicides and their causes. Thompson, while in San Antonio, went into a gambling house owned by Jack Harris, Joe Foster, Billy Simms, and probably some others. Ben had lost heavily and had pledged his jewelry to the gambling house. The jewelry consisted of some very valuable

diamonds. He had been robbed, without any chance of winning, and being in the mood that losers generally get into under such circumstances, he went to the gambling house and took his diamonds again into his possession at the point of his pistol, using language that was pretty forcible, in fact, cursed the whole house, and denounced them as thieves. Jack Harris, one of the firm, was a man of violent temper, and Thompson's action irritated him to such an extent that he was ready at any time for a difficulty with Thompson. Thus matters stood when Ben went to San Antonio, and he and Jack Harris met face-to-face, Ben on the sidewalk in front and Harris inside the vaudeville theater, with a shotgun in his hands. Harris was killed in the act of getting his gun in position to shoot Thompson. The main witnesses for the prosecution in the Harris-Thompson case were Billy Simms and Joe Foster, and what money was needed in the prosecution was said to have been furnished them. The trial was long and bitter, and it intensified the feeling on both sides. Consequently the parties to the tragedy of Tuesday night in San Antonio had every reason to believe that fresh trouble would arise should circumstances present the opportunity. The devilish opportunity was presented, and our readers are already aware of the result.

Mrs. Irene Bundrick lived in Superior, Montana, and recalled payday in the 1890s, "On paydays, Pardee boomed. The grocery store was in the same room with a saloon, at the back of the building. I was sometimes sent for groceries, and I often saw stacks of gold a foot high on the counter. Money clinked in poker games, the miners too busy with their gambling to notice me. Buckskin pokes were used to carry nuggets of different sizes, and ounce or two-ounce bottles for gold dust brought out from Cedar Creek. I remember seeing Bill Bonnett, Al Wade, and Tom Mulroney turning these over to the grocer to weigh."

The gambling scene could be a frenzied one. One man, Mike "Red Mike" Ryan, of Tombstone, Arizona, found out just how dangerous that could be. Mike was no saint himself, and he had been released from jail in early July 1881 after being held six months awaiting trial on an attempted murder charge. On July 14, Mike became slightly intoxicated and roamed the streets of Tombstone with a great roll of greenbacks in his hand. Mike offered to bet anyone from five cents to a thousand dollars on the ace "straight up." As the night wore on, Mike became more inebriated and eventually leaned against an adobe wall half asleep. Three "sharks" approached Ryan, and upon seeing this, City Marshal and Chief of Police Virgil Earp brought Ryan into custody. Earp took $230 from Ryan's overalls for safekeeping, put him to bed, and released him in the morning.

The gambling scene could be a frenzied one. One man, Mike "Red Mike" Ryan, of Tombstone, Arizona, found out just how dangerous that could be.

After his narrow escape from the sharks, Ryan realized Earp had not found all his money. Since Ryan's money was burning a hole in his pocket, he decided to "blow it in" in good style. Calling upon everyone he saw in the Golden Eagle Brewery, he invited them "to toss the ruby." As willing participants surrounded him, Mike was "jostled," and thieves took two $100 bills. The perpetrators clumsily committed their crime and were seen by a dozen or so witnesses who easily identified them. A warrant was sworn out for William Freeman, alias "Red Billy," and his accomplice, Jim Bennet, shortly after they committed the crime. Red Billy hired a team of horses with his newfound fortune and set out for Charleston. The deputy sheriff in Charleston received the dispatch too late from Tombstone to catch the crook, and "Red Billy" headed for Benson. Virgil Earp telegraphed his brother, Morgan, who was in Benson at the time. It was again too late; "Red Billy" boarded the train.

Marshal Earp arrested Red Billy's partner-in-crime, Jim Bennet, after he tried to get a $100 bill changed at one of the feed corrals. Red Billy eventually joined his partner when Morgan Earp arrested him in Benson and returned him to Tombstone. Bennet was later acquitted for lack of evidence, and "Red Billy" skipped town for parts unknown.

The *Daily Nugget* deemed Mike Ryan a "persistent offender" after he became involved in yet another incident. Since the Golden Eagle Brewery previously proved a "hostile" environment for Mike, he chose to take his business to Lou Rickabaugh's Oriental clubrooms. The Oriental proved just as bad for Mike, but this time from his own doing. For reasons unknown, he helped himself to a twenty-dollar piece from one of the faro table draws.

Ryan was promptly arrested and taken to the city jail by Marshal Earp. Earp later brought in a "fellow full of joy" and put him in the cell with Ryan. About an hour later, as Earp took Ryan to the county jail, Ryan suggested he and the chief stop in for a drink somewhere. Earp replied, "On what? You haven't a cent."

"Ain't I though?" said Ryan. "What do you call that?" He showed Earp four bits and a ten-cent piece. When asked where he got the money, Ryan informed the chief he had rolled his cellmate and found it! Ryan was arraigned and taken before Judge Wallace on July 19, whereupon he pled "not guilty" and demanded a jury. Mike claimed he did not roll his cellmate and claimed Marshal Earp had lied.

The game of poker is currently enjoying a huge comeback, but today's popularity can't compare with bygone days. Though most of the larger saloons specialized in faro, monte, and roulette, poker was a regular feature of the gambling scene and very popular in smaller towns and cow camps. It required no special equipment, and games could be "got up" quickly and sometimes went on for days.

The Wicked West

E. F. Forsgard of Waco, Texas, reminisced, "Four or five or six of these big gamblers would sometimes get together in one of their places and play poker. Sometimes the game would run for as long as a week. If one of them wanted to leave the game for awhile to take a nap or go out in town, he'd count up the money he had, the banker would make a note of it, and the gambler would stack it to one side on the table, and it would be there when he came back, even if he was gone a day or two. A lot of gambling would go on right on the square. The cowboys, gamblers, and Mexicans would come into town and tie their horses to the hitch rack on the square, spread down a blanket, get out their cards, and have a game right there among their horses."

John Raines immigrated to Tarrant County, Texas, with his father

The acoutrements of a gentleman gambler—including a mustache-curling iron. (Objects courtesy of Tombstone Western Heritage Museum.)

in 1875 near Fort Worth. He recalled his ranch-hand days during the 1870s and 1880s: "Those days, Fort Worth was surrounded by cow outfits, with a few farms scattered here and there. Any day of the week, and especially Saturdays, the streets were dotted with waddies swaggering with their attire of chaps, guns, and J. B. Stetson hats. Without those parts of the cowhand's outfit, he was undressed. Most all of the waddies were looking for some fun and generally found it any form they desired. While at camp, the boss spent their off hours in various ways, but cards held the first place as a method of entertainment. There were some mighty good gamblers among the cowhands. Our cook was the best poker player in our outfit. When he came into town

When the big gamblers got together, the game might go on for a week.

for a spell of recreation a poker game was what he hunted for. I know of one winning of $3,000 he pulled down one Saturday night. However, he never held onto his winnings, because he couldn't resist the roulette wheel. At the roulette wheel, he couldn't out-guess the wheel and little ball as he could a man holding a poker hand."

Faro was one of the most favored banking games in the Wild West. Businessmen, cattle drovers, and miners often visited saloons to "buck the tiger," an expression thought to stem from the fact that old playing cards had tigers on the back, and if you won, you bucked the tiger.

When played without cheating, faro was called the "gentlemen's game." Given a square deal, the percentage against the player and in favor of the bank was less than any other game of its kind. If it was not dealt fairly, as was often the case, a gambler had no more chance than "a cat in Hades without claws," according to Tombstone, Arizona's July 22, 1881, *Daily Nugget*.

Rules of Faro

Equipment

Faro layout A "faro layout" is essential. It consists of cards glued on a board that may have folded together from each side into the middle. The layout itself, usually covered with green cloth or felt, is similar to that used on billiard tables. It includes all of the spades and is laid out as such, from left to right:

Top row: King, Queen, Jack, Ten, Nine, Eight
                                                Seven
Bottom row: Ace, Two, Three, Four, Five, Six

52-card deck Any deck will do. Decks in the Old West did not have numbers on them.

Cue box or case keeper (optional) A cue box is used to keep track of which cards have already been played. It was monitored by a "look-out." Players may also use a sheet of paper.

Card box (optional) A card box is used to hold the cards face up, but this is not necessary. The cards may simply be placed on the table.

Chips (optional) Poker chips are the traditional betting piece for the game, but coins may be used instead. Pennies are also needed for coppering bets (*see the rules below for an explanation of this*).

To play the game: Shuffle the cards and cut the deck. The dealer's deck is placed face up on the table or in a card box. Before any cards are dealt, all bets must be placed by marking one of the spades or a combination of them with a chip or check. When the cards are shuffled and placed face up on the table, the first card appearing is called the "soda" card and is placed in a discard pile. The following rules will be based on not using a box, since most playing this game at home will not have one. While spades are used on the layout, suits are irrelevant in this game, and only the denomination matters.

The soda card is laid to the dealer's far right and away from the deck. The next card to appear is the losing card, and it is placed directly next to the deck. The card appearing on the deck is the winning card. For example, a player places a chip on the three to win. The dealer turns the first card, a king, which is the losing card, and then turns the second card, a four, which is the winning card. Since the player did not choose the four or the king, they neither win nor lose. The dealer would collect all bets placed on the losing card, and pay any bets on the winning card. That concludes a turn. Bets can be left where they were made, they can be moved, or new bets may be placed again. The winning card—in this example, the king—now becomes a soda card, and is placed in that pile. Again, the next card to appear is the losing card, and it is placed directly next to the deck. The card appearing on the deck is once again the winner. There is no real end to the game, and it can continue indefinitely. If the cards run out, they can be shuffled and play resumes.

If a player thinks a certain card will lose, he can "copper" his stack of chips, which indicates he is betting to lose. To copper, simply place a penny on the bet covering the card to lose. For example, a player places a copper on his $1 bet covering the king. The dealer turns the first card, a king, which is the losing card, and then turns the second card, a four, which is the winning card. Since the player chose the king to lose, he wins the bet. That also concludes a turn.

Bets can be placed in many different positions on the layout, and the way they are placed determines how the hand goes. For example, if a player puts a stack of chips between the king and the queen (or any other two cards) and puts a "copper" on the king, he bets the king will lose and the queen will win. If the cards come out and both are against him, he is "whip-sawed" on the turn and loses. Bets can also be placed behind three cards, on the corners between two, or in any position that will take in any of the combinations that are allowed in the game.

Bets are paid dollar for dollar. If you bet one dollar, you get one back.

Whenever the winning and losing card are of the same value (i.e., a six and a six), or if the player has wagered the same bet on two cards, then the dealer only takes half of the bet. If the amount cannot be divided evenly, then the difference belongs to the dealer.

In addition to the regular bets, players have the choice of "calling the turn" when the last three cards are left (there are actually four cards left, but the top card will be discarded as the soda). A player can try to guess in which order the last three cards will be dealt. Once bets are placed (which should be easy if players kept track of the cards already played) a player can call the turn. If successful, they are paid four to one; if not, they lose. The trick to calling the play is guessing in which order the last three cards will be drawn. There are six different combinations.

If two of the last three cards are the same, (i.e., two fives and one jack appear) it's called a cat-hop, and the dealer pays two to one.

The dealer collects any remaining bets on the table.

A former San Simon, Arizona, rancher named John C. Hancock described the game as it was played during the late 1800s:

> The fellow with the gun at the end of the table looks very comical, but is entirely out of place as the look-out. The look-out does not pay off or take in the bets—the dealer does that after he makes the turn, as it is called. There is an old saying among faro dealers, and also those that like to "buck" the game, that if a blackjack appears as the "soda" card, the seven will win throughout the game; however, many have found out that it is only a superstitious saying.
>
> A "case keeper" sat opposite the dealer with a little box. On the little box, in the center lengthways and along the hinges that were in the center, were miniature pictures of the cards themselves. The little wire led from the picture of the card to the edge of the case on which were strung four small disks. As cards were dealt out, the case keeper moved these disks in such a way that a new player joining the game could glance at the cases and tell what cards had lost and how they were dealt out of the box. If the game was dealt fairly, or "on the square," it gave even odds, or was supposed to, but the bank nearly always came out the winner in the long run. The bank paid even money on all bets but the last turn.
>
> In addition to the dealer, a "look-out" can occupy a slightly elevated seat either at the right or left of the dealer, whichever is convenient. A look-out oversaw the game, watched all bets and looked for any mistakes made during the deal. When a big game was played and the layout was covered with bets, placed in all manners of ways in combinations, the look-out had to pay strict attention to the game.

Rules of Monte

Equipment

Money As much as you dare to lose.

Deck of cards Any standard deck will do. Remove the eights, nines, and tens.

Terminology

Banker Dealer

Punter Player

To play the game (according to *The American Hoyle,* 1880, and *Hoyle's Games,* 1907): There are no set bets in monte, and the game is played until the dealer runs out of cash. Players win even money. Start by shuffling the cards. The dealer takes two cards from the bottom of the deck and places them on the table, face up. These are called the bottom layout. The dealer takes two cards from the top of the deck and places them face up, above the other two cards. They are called the top layout. Players place their bets on the card or cards on either layout.

Players are betting on which suit will match the one shown by the dealer. The card's number is irrelevant, and only the suit matters. Once the bets are placed, the dealer turns the deck over to expose the bottom card or the "gate" or "port" card. Any bets placed on the suit that matches that card, wins. All others lose. For example:

Top layout:	2 ♠ & King ♥
Bottom layout:	4 ♦ & Jack ♠

Dealer's bottom card: any ♣ = everyone loses and the dealer collects all bets.

> If the dealer's card was any ♥ = whoever placed their bet on the heart won.
>
> Since there are no clubs showing, the dealer would win the hand. Any bets placed on the heart would win. That concludes the hand.

When Deadwood, South Dakota, was in full swing in the 1870s and 1880s, faro games were available throughout the city. One local citizen, Dr. Bagg, tackled a faro dealer with $.50, and took $100. Another placed a faro check worth $3.25 in the church collection plate. In the nearby town of Lead, Ira Kilgore opened a faro game with disastrous results. The players won amounts ranging from $25 to $200, until Ira, disgusted, turned over the box.

Monte was another popular saloon game in the Old West and was considered the national game of Mexico in 1880. It was played with Spanish cards, which were thinner than other cards and numbered forty (lacking the eights, nines, and tens). The dealer or banker had to display his entire money that he intends to risk that night in plain sight on the table. Monte or Spanish monte was played extensively in the American Southwest and was especially popular with the Mexican and Indian populations. The game attained its greatest popularity among whites during the California gold rush. Most saloons offered monte, and it remained a popular banking game throughout the nineteenth century. Monte was also a game that often included very high stakes, which were favored by the era's "high rollers."

Bud Brown ran a saloon in Colorado City, Texas in the 1880s. He fondly remembered his life then: "Gambling was one of the diversions, and all the popular games were operated to accommodate the cowhands. To present an idea of the extent the boys played, I shall tell about a game Clay Mann was engaged in. Bob Winders was one of the monte dealers, and an excellent one. Mann came in one day and looked over the stack of $20-gold coins stacked on the table. The coins covered a space about one foot square and were stacked about six inches high. Bob was running the cards and had turned up a jack. Clay Mann said, 'Bob, I want to bet a mule's tail and some coin on that jack.' 'Alright, Clay,' Bob said, 'lay out what it takes to talk.' Clay reached in his shirt bosom and pulled out two sacks of money, which he emptied in his ten-gallon

Western high rollers might encounter any number of distractions designed to put them off their game.

hat, so the money could be easier reached. The hat's crown was almost full of gold coins. The time was about 1 p.m. when Clay and Bob began to play monte, and Clay played steadily till 12 o'clock. Several times he went out for sandwiches and would occasionally send for a drink from the bar. At one time Clay was close to a $10,000-winner and at another time he was about the same amount a loser. However, when Clay quit he was a $100-winner. Games such as Clay played were not unusual in those days, and losses and winnings often ran into the thousands."

Being a monte dealer in a saloon proved costly one for man in west Texas. W. W. Adney recalled: "When I was driving a freight wagon, I came in with the Word boys and unloaded at the fort. We had some money, so we decided to have some fun. We made straight for the Gray

Mule Saloon. Rocky Rivers was proprietor of the saloon, and that night he was tending bar …. There were about three hundred fellows there—Negroes, whites, soldiers, gamblers—everything was in that building. About midnight a big fight started. The lights were put out, and six-shooters began to pop. I grabbed my gun, dropped to the floor, and rolled under the counter. The only light came from those popping six-shooters. After the shooting stopped and the smoke began clearing, Rocky called for lights. With the first light, Rocky saw my feet sticking out from under the counter. He jerked out a gun in each hand and covered me, but just about then, he could see my face. 'That you, kid?' he inquired calmly, 'Just stay right where you are.' Three men were wounded, a monte dealer, a soldier, and another man, but none were killed. By then I told the boys that I had already had enough fun for a while."

Keno was a popular game in the West as well. Saloons everywhere advertised keno pots. Keno isn't a traditional banking game played with a deck of cards, but rather players buy as many cards as they like and then lay them down in any arrangement in rows on the table. Similar to modern games of bingo, ninety numbered balls are tumbled in a "goose," or basket. Balls are then drawn from the goose. As a player's card is drawn, he lays a button on it. The first player to get five of his cards in a horizontal row shouts "keno." Once confirmed, the player wins the pot.

According to ethnographer Stewart Cullen, keno is probably derived from a much older Chinese game first established in the great Han dynasty, which encouraged participants to gamble away their property to the empire. When the game was first established, the houses were often at a great distance, and people were anxious to know the result respecting their gains and losses. Thus, they employed letter doves to carry the news, and keno has also been called "The Game of the White Dove."

In the West, the game thrived among Chinese immigrants, especially around big cities such as San Francisco, where it became known as the Chinese lottery. English-speaking Americans became interested in the game, but had difficulty differentiating the Chinese characters used in the game. Around the beginning of the twentieth century, keno operators replaced the Chinese characters with Arabic numbers to entice more players. Gus's saloon in Tombstone, Arizona, did a good business. He offered keno every night, and gave away $2.50 with the first pot and $2.50 at nine o'clock every night.

The expression "tin-horn" gambler originated with a certain class of gamblers whose stock in trade consisted of a cone-shaped tin tube. Several pieces of heavy wire were fastened across the inside of it, and dice were thrown through the small end of the tube. The dice struck the wires and were tossed about until landing on the table. The players then guessed what was shown on the dice, whereupon the tin tube was lifted, and the results were revealed.

According to New Mexico's *Silver City Enterprise:*

> From the fact of it being a game that serves to attract only petty players, it is generally referred to with contempt by genuine gambling men, and the individual running it is called "tin-horn" gambler. From this the expression had spread and been adopted into the vernacular of the West until now it is used to designate all classes of individuals who profess to follow a kind of business, of which in reality they know but little.
>
> Consequently, we hear of "tin-horn" capitalists, mining men, stock men, lawyers, doctors, etc., and there are also "tin-horn" newspapermen. The newspaper "tin-horn" is usually what is termed a "smart Aleck" and delights in feeble attempts at wit, at the expense of others. He will pick up some commonplace remark and endeavor in his witless way to make much of it, to the disgust of sensible people. This is not an advertisement, but simply the private opinions

of a trained newspaper man concerning "tin-horn" editors and reporters, a few of whom, if the truth must be told, find by some inscrutable way that means of livelihood.

Saloons interested in creating a more diverse gambling environment could install their own roulette wheels, as at least a few proprietors in Fort Worth did. Andre Jorgensen Anderson, who operated a gun store in town, also happened to do some gunsmithing and particular mechanical work, and he knew the roulette wheels well. "I was called on for repairing gambling devices. The roulette table contains a number of numbered compartments into which a small ball drops after spinning around the wheel. These compartments are just large enough to receive the ball. The bottom of a major part of these compartments was fixed so as to be movable and could be raised slightly. The operation of the compartment floors was done by means of a small lever and wire cables, which were concealed. These wires ran to the floor. The device was manipulated with the feet of the gaming operator. It was these devices, and others, which I repaired. Suppose a heavy bet was made on the double 0. If the ball started to drop into the double 0 compartment, manipulation of the section's floor would cause the ball to roll to the adjacent compartment. The only way a player could win was for the operator to become paralyzed in his feet, and I never knew of such to happen. Once in a while one would hear of some fellow winning a large stake, but generally it was some party connected with the gambling business, and the

> **Saloons interested in creating a more diverse gambling environment could install their own roulette wheels...**

winning act was put on for advertising purposes. Frequently, a player would be allowed to win a small amount, and this was done to encourage the players."

Another Fort Worth resident, John Raines, recalled a roulette wheel experience during the 1870s and 1880s: "Fatty thought he had solved the mystery of the wheel one time, but it proved to be a fluke. He came into town one payday and went straight to a roulette game. It was about mid-day when he sit down to play. The next day at noon he was playing still and sitting on the same stool he started on. He had never stopped long enough for his meals— those were brought to him and he ate while playing. I had left Fatty playing that payday, and when he failed to drag into camp by the following morning ... it darkened our cloud to have our swell belly-cheater gone, and it caused one of the cowhands to do the cooking. So I dragged into town to see what was the trouble. Well, there I found him shoving in chips and hauling some back occasionally. At that time it was estimated that he had close to $5,000 stacked around him. He then was so sleepy that he was taking a drink of liquor about every thirty minutes to keep himself going. I tried to have Fatty cash in and come home with me, but I failed to get him in that mood. I said to him, 'Fatty you are going to sit there till you're broke or fall off that seat.' He just grunted and kept on playing. He started with his month's wages, except a few he may have spent for clothes. I calculated $5,000 was a good winning, but not Fatty. I left him at the roulette table and told him I would return in a couple hours. I reckoned that was about the limit of time he could stay awake. When I returned, he was leaving the table and the professor was handing Fatty $1 to buy 'baccy or eats before starting back to camp. Fatty had lost all of his winnings. The next day at camp we waddies were cussing Fatty for not quitting the game while he was $5,000 to the good. His answer was, 'Hell boys, I had $100-worth of fun out of my month's pay.'"

North Dakota's Harry Buffington Cody (called "Buffalo Cody" by his friends because of his relationship with Buffalo Bill and his middle name, Buffington) was employed in 1888 on Buffalo Bill's Wild West Show until 1890, at which time he established a show of his own. Cody recalled his experience with roulette.

> I had a little over $900, and I wanted to invest it in some kind of a game and run it way up. After looking around and sweating all the games going on, and there was a many a one, I decided on roulette. I'll never forget how lucky I got in that old Peacock Saloon and Bar. It was a regular palace, with all its mirrors and so on, its women that were dressed in velvet what part the dress covered they were, and everything else. There was even a 40-foot bar, of which I've seen them longer and bigger since, but that was a monster for them days. Men going around in shabby clothes, as I was, and some of them carrying fortunes with them. No telling what percentage of this money found its way into the crooked hands that were there, but I'll guarantee you that a bigger percentage than most people think must have gone there ... bigger honest-to-God sucker game than roulette never was, but I thought I could make on it. I didn't even have a combination, nor a set of lucky numbers. I just hopped around over the board, here and there, and nearly every time I hopped, I won. I sure got a lot of hard looks too, because some of the men in the crowd followed my bets, and put their own with mine. That away, when I won, they won. After sticking with them dirty crooks for two solid days, leaving only for a few minutes at a time, I walked out of that big old Peacock with $5,000 to the good. I didn't leave, though, 'til the marshal told me he'd take care of me and I'd better leave while I was so far ahead. My luck had attracted most everybody in town, and I reckon they done a lot of extra business just on the strength of what I was

doing, but they didn't want me to get out of there with all that dinero.

Now, just a marshal didn't mean a thing to that kind of people, but Wild Bill Hickock did, and he was the marshal, being appointed to keep order there by General Sheridan, who ran the military post there. He took my money and gave me a receipt for it, telling me that any time I got ready to leave, I could have it. He also let word get around that anything that happened to me, happened to his friend, and he wouldn't like it. He sure was one more real man.

Not all forms of gambling involved tables set up in saloon corners. One in particular, while enormously popular, was not considered "socially" acceptable. Nevertheless, on Sunday afternoons many male Tombstonians didn't hesitate to head into back streets and various other places to place bets and watch feisty yard birds attack each other in cockfights. Ike Isaacs, a well-known faro dealer, was also noted for his game-chicken expertise. He claimed Tombstone had more first-class game chickens than any other place in America, since almost everyone owned one. A grand match was held in Schieffelin Hall during the month of August in 1881. Hopeful participants were encouraged to leave their address with Bob Hatch of Campbell's & Hatch's Saloon or at the Belliona parlors.

Albert Young and William Bobier, who lived two miles out of town, were two of the main suppliers of Tombstone's prized fighting cocks. Young was a sixty-seven-year-old from Kentucky, while Bobier, about fifty, hailed from Sherman, Texas. The birds were descended from prestigious Kentucky stock. The men raised the birds on their farm, in addition to growing vegetables, which they sold in Tombstone's markets. One particularly hot Sunday afternoon in July proved fatal, not for the birds, but for one of their owners. It seems that Young and Bobier had sold one of their birds to a Tombstone businessman. This businessman showed up on Sunday with his new bird and challenged Young and Bobier's bird. Young refereed the fight, and Bobier handled the bird.

After much argument, it was conceded that Young and Bobier's bird lost by a technicality. The decision fell to the referee, who declared it a draw; all bets were called off. Bobier was not happy and threatened to kill Young for his decision. As the two men walked home together after the fight, Bobier began hurling insults at Young, threatening to kill him. Then he switched from words to fists. He punched Young in the ear, knocking him to the ground. Continuing to assault Young, Bobier picked up a large rock. As Young began to run he drew his 22-caliber pistol and fired behind him to scare Bobier, not realizing that his shot hit Bobier in the heart, and he died instantly. At the coroner's inquest, Young was exonerated from any wrong doing, mainly because Bobier was known to be quarrelsome, had been drunk, and had previously threatened to kill Young.

Toward the end of the nineteenth century, Fort Worth's White Elephant saloon offered purses of up to $2,000 for cockfighting, and Texas also had its share of cockfights. Lee D. Leverett remained on his father's farm until he was twenty-one years old, then went to the Indian Territory (now Oklahoma) to work for the Graham Ranch, located near the town of Duncan. He remembered a story told by an old-timer on the ranch: "The cleanest lie I ever heard was told by Bob Shank. He was an old-timer and had nested on many outfits all over the Southwest. Let me give you that tale, the best I can, as he told it: 'I was nesting with an outfit down on the border, before the Civil War. The ramrod got an idea in his conk to move his outfit into a valley country across the Rio Grande. So we drifted the critters into the country and got nicely settled. There were several vaqueros in the out-fit and them fellows are set on having their cockfights. They had several cocks that they took along, and they fixed a run for the birds next to a spring where the birds had plenty of fresh water. After the runs were fixed, the birds were placed in the pens and at once started to scratch for worms and other food. It wasn't long until those birds were trying to break out of the runs. The Mexican vaqueros pronto got busy to see what all the fuss was about. You may not believe it, but the facts are that a large number of worms were chasing hell out of those fighting birds.'"

Chapter 6

The Red-Light Ladies

S OCIAL LIFE IN MANY BOOMTOWNS was a topsy-turvy mix of hard-bitten ramblers, the suddenly wealthy, and the professional drinkers and gamblers who followed the money. In many new towns, "respectable" female companionship was hard to come by, and men were far from their homes and families—if they had them at all. Women who were unwilling, or forbidden, to work alongside men in frontier industries often resorted to prostitution to make ends meet.

For some, it was a true profession, and they would travel from town to town as fortunes and fashions shifted. If they had money, they might set up a house of their own and manage other "red-light ladies." For others, the line was more ambiguous. Did an impoverished woman who cultivated her friendship with a mine foreman count as a prostitute? Complicating the issue, the concept of marriage was often loosely interpreted in the Old West to explain the relationships that might spring up on the edges of civilization.

Nevertheless, prostitution was a part of the social fabric in most Western towns. It was usually connected to lower-class saloons or dance halls, where lonely men went to seek female companionship. The account of Fort Worth resident Andre Jorgensen Anderson shows just how fluidly one form of entertainment led into another: "The theater called the Centennial was run by a man named Low. It was located at about Eleventh and Rusk (now Commerce) Streets, and was one of the major attractions of the town during the period from the middle '70s to the early '80s. Low was a man about six feet tall, weighing about 180 pounds, with an excellent physique. I can best describe the man by saying he was an Adonis-type man. Low always dressed immaculately and wore expensive jewelry with diamonds being conspicuous .... He made frequent trips visiting other saloons and treated the crowd. Also, he was liberal with donations to charity and to public subscriptions for various purposes. On the ground floor was the bar and dance hall. The dancing floor was in the center of the room. The theater was at the rear of the bar and dance hall.

Gambling was operated on the second floor. Also, the rooms occupied by the actresses were located on the second floor. Above the first floor was a gallery, extending around the major part of the room. The actresses would sit in the gallery when not engaged in their acts on the stage. The acts were of the scurrilous type, very suggestive, and for men only. No ladies would attend the theater unless disguised, which many did and enjoyed the show. The customers, mostly cowboys, would visit the actresses in the gallery.

Lillian Russell was one of the girls who made good, going on to become an actress and companion to the famous gambler Diamond Jim Brady.

THE RED-LIGHT LADIES

These women had a system of selling their visitors a key to their room. If one bought a key, he would have the privilege of treating the actress in her room, paying $1 a bottle for beer and other drinks at the same rate in price, and be undisturbed during the visit."

Some women may have preferred the social freedom they gained from being a professional and some were attracted by the excitement of the mining camps and cow towns. If a woman on her own was really lucky, she might meet a man and live a respectable life. Still others viewed prostitution as one of the few professions where women had a chance of financial success.

At least one such woman was remembered with awe in Canyon City, Oregon. It may have been a remote town in the late 1860s, but it certainly provided a great deal of entertainment. Its residents were also quite colorful. Mrs. Minnie Clark-Ford, who was the second child born in Canyon City, vividly remembered some of the life and residents: "Perhaps the most noted hell-raiser in the history of Canyon City was Marie St. Claire—the wildest, toughest, and most beautiful light woman the houses there ever had. Marie was kind and generous to everyone. If crossed, though, she could draw and plug her man with the best of them. I remember that she would go horseback riding in men's clothes; something no lady, scarcely a light one, would do. When she dressed in her gorgeous velvet dresses she could dazzle anyone. Marie lived extravagantly. Her home had every luxury known to the world at that time. Her silver service was particularly beautiful. Wild, beautiful, dangerous Marie St. Claire had the secret admiration of everyone, despite her profession."

For others, keeping an eye on the "sporting ladies" really was something of a sport in itself. William "Billy" Mayer of Oregon reminisced about such women fondly. "In Portland is a notorious locality, known by the suggestive name of the 'White-Chapel District.' It is the home of the most abandoned members of the *demimonde*, and on a small scale resembles the famous section of London, after which it

⇥ PORTLAND'S *SPORTING HOUSE GUIDE* ⇤

This in a guide without avarice tainted
A "tip," as it were, before you're acquainted.
And now, my good friends, you've had my excuse;
I could have said more, but what is the use?
This thing I've "writ" and it is dedicated
To strangers and those who're uninitiated.

MISS MINNIE REYNOLDS 89 Fifth Street
In handsome parlors, skilled to please,
Fair Minnie waits in silken ease,
And at each guest's desire supplies
Dear pleasures, hid from prying eyes.
With such a haven ever nigh,
Who could pass her parlors by?

MISS FANSHAW 151 Seventh Street
Let's live while we live;
We'll be dead a long while,
And tho Fortune may frown,
Fair Miss Fanshaw will smile.
If a kiss will not soothe you,
She has pleasures that will;
The chalice of passion overflowingly fill,
And your troubles and cares
You will lightly ignore
When love's rich libation
This charmer will pour.

MISS MABEL MONTAGUE 94 Fifth Street, Cor. Stark
Here is a mansion, of which it is related
That on all of this Coast it is not duplicated.
Its well-furnished parlors the fashionable seek,
For comfort is here, joined to the unique,
And the girls who respond to the visitors' call,
Are the pride of Miss Mabel, and the pride of her hall.

MISS DORA CLARK & MISS MAUD MORRISON
95 Sixth Street, Cor. Stark
No man in this City who is known as a sport
But will tell you he's seen and enjoyed this resort.
It's a house full of beauties, whose rooms dazzling bright,
Shimmer and glimmer with mirth and delight.

DORA LYNN
If you're out for a lark, or that is your passion,
Just call at this house, so lately in fashion.
With its fairylike nymphs and Dora Lynn its queen,
Where privacy, rest, and all is serene.
There are a great many Doras, but I write this one down
As the best one that ever has lived in this town.

is named. Within its boundaries are several hundred women, most of whom live in small one-story houses or cribs. The inmates of these cribs represent every nationality, with the French predominating. On Lower Second Street can be seen Japanese and African women. This district lies north of Ankeny Street, and, owing to the surveillance of Portland's admirable police department, is perfectly safe for the stranger to visit, provided he does not get too familiar with the occupants of the 'cribs.'"

The Wicked West

Mayer kept a copy of the *Sporting House Guide* for Portland in the gay 90s. A sporting house guide included listings for some of Portland's prostitutes with some unusual advertising—poetry. Mayer said, "Here, these verses—Sam Simpson, the old poet of Oregon, is said to have written them; I don't know. But they advertised the 'madams.' Yes, they were all called 'madam' then. I don't know why they all have 'Miss' in front of their names here."

Some "red-light ladies" either hid or tried to keep their occupation a secret from family or relatives. Some even listed their occupations as actress on the census in order to hide their profession. Irene Bundrick, a resident of Superior, Montana, remembered one prostitute struggling to raise her child without giving away the secret of her income. "And we couldn't shut our eyes to Minnie, the prostitute; the flaming red Mother Hubbard she affected was too easily recognized at a distance. Like the others of her profession here at that time, she was not very young; cross-eyes marred her appearance. She had a child whom she kept in a school, ignorant of the mother's means of livelihood."

In fact, these women attracted little notice in their business unless they overstepped the invisible lines that divided them from respectable citizens. Virginia City, Nevada, for example, had its share of soiled doves. Their places were called "disorderly houses" or "shebangs." When the town was in full swing, the ladies of ill-fame were numerous. They had cribs or houses on South C Street and D Street, with others scattered about town. The red-light district in Virginia City was called the "Barbary Coast." Most of the "ladies" were content to ply their trade quietly, but some always seemed to be in trouble. A madam by the name of Mrs. Cochran made the news in November 1875 when she was arrested for disturbing the peace and selling liquor without a license. Two other town members were arrested in conjunction with the disturbing the peace charge—Mr. Wilson and Mr. Kearney.

Nellie Sayers, once a notorious member of Virginia City's *demi-monde*, made frequent news. One of her biggest stories involved a man by the name of Peter Larkin, with whom she was living on C Street. On March 4, 1875, Virginia City awoke to a gunshot at 6:30 a.m. Larkin owned what the locals called "a low drinking saloon." It seems Nellie and Peter, after much quarreling, finally separated. Larkin went to San Francisco, and upon his return, brought with him a young good-looking woman named Susie Brown. Undisturbed, Nellie opened a saloon next door to Larkin's, so close that they could see in each other's windows. As the story goes, Larkin never got over Nellie, so when he saw her with a new amour, Daniel Corcoran, he was beside himself with jealousy. The Gold Hill, Nevada's *Evening News* wrote, "Corcoran, a fat, good-natured, ignorant Irishman, appeared upon the scene ... and rows between the rival gin mills became frequent." Eventually Susie Brown became tired of the fighting and her lover's obvious affection for Nellie. Giving the tale a further twist, Susie moved into Nellie's house. Poor Larkin couldn't take it anymore and decided to put an end to Nellie's affair with Corcoran. Early that fateful morning, Larkin entered

To some, bordello tokens were more valuable than gamblers' chips.

Nellie's saloon. Corcoran heard a noise and went into the bar to check it out. Larkin shot Corcoran in the stomach, and he died the next day. After a long trial and eighteen months in jail, Larkin was finally hanged in a very public show.

The Wicked West

The papers had a field day, mostly at Nellie's expense. According to the *Evening News*, "A more unattractive female could scarcely exist. Low, ignorant, and drunken, and devoid of all personal charms, who was yet so valuable in the eyes of two men that gave their lives for her."

On April 5, 1877, the Virginia City, Nevada, *Territorial Enterprise* reported a story entitled "Disorderly Houses." It began, "Warrants were last evening issued on complaints made, and Miss Nellie Sayers and Mrs. Corcoran were arrested by Constable Norton and taken in before judge Moses for keeping disorderly houses." The following day the *Territorial Enterprise* reported that Mrs. Corcoran pled guilty to her charge and was fined $1 and court costs. Nellie Sayers preferred to fight her charge and demanded a jury to try her case. The paper wrote, "She doubtless hopes to ring one or more of her 'friends' in on the jury, so as to procure a disagreement, if not an acquittal. This city and county have borne very much from this woman, but that does not forfeit her rights to a fair and impartial trial, which she will doubtless have before Judge Moses." While Nellie did not win this case, she continued to ply her trade. In June of the same year the paper reported, "From keeper of a house of common prostitution she has descended to still lower depths of infamy, and became proprietress of a den of deeper disgrace, and is acting as procuress, for the

Although this picture is from a cigarette ad, sporting ladies also often enticed their customers with exotic costumes.

frequenters of her place, but little girls, who are there drugged with vile liquors and given over to debauchery." They also reported that Nellie had been arrested repeatedly but managed to escape conviction, except of keeping a disorderly house. Her license to sell liquors was revoked, but even that did not affect her business.

When such women were arrested, their treatment depended on their connections as much as any conception of justice. For example, in Tombstone, Mrs. McDonald was brought in for keeping a house of ill fame, and so was Tombstone's notorious Miss Emma Parker. Both ladies pled "not guilty" and were held over for trial. Mrs. McDonald, dubbed the "much persecuted lady of ill fame," found only one friendly face among her twelve male jurors. Unable to agree on a unanimous decision, the jury was discharged to give the court, officers, and attorneys an opportunity to go over details. Just what happened to the charges against Miss Parker and Mrs. McDonald is unclear. What is clear, though, is that Emma Parker was not content to live her life in Tombstone unnoticed. A few days after being brought in on charges of keeping a house of ill fame, Emma got into still more trouble. She entered the Occidental Saloon about half-past one in the morning and began arguing with bartender and owner Gus Williams, becoming so unruly she was arrested. Emma did not go quietly, and her screams aroused everyone in the neighborhood. She was booked for being drunk and disorderly, using vulgar language, and fighting.

When not brought under official scrutiny, prostitutes moved freely through their world and just as often drifted away. As quickly as red-light districts sprang up, they might disappear. Just two years after all the press over Nellie Sayers, in July 1887, Virginia City's *Territorial Enterprise* declared the notorious Barbary Coast was no more. A town cleanup, prompted by a need for more real estate, had forced the *demimondes* to relocate. As towns grew more refined, shady ladies were often forced to move on or find other ways to make a living. Since the average age of them was in the mid-twenties, they had a chance of starting over in a new town or even marrying. Some did, but others ended up living in poverty or not living at all.

As with any profession, there was a certain social hierarchy among the red-light ladies. Brothel owners and the girls who worked in the better establishments generally scorned the dance-hall girls who rented rooms over buildings and tended to operate independently.

Julia Bullette was Virginia City's most famous madam. After she was found murdered in her bed, thousands of men and boys marched in her funeral procession.

Montana saloon owner George Fowlie recalled some dance halls and saloons he saw while living out West. Fowlie's saloon was in Castle, Montana, at the corner of Main and Castle. Before entering into the saloon business though, George was a school principal in Phillips, Wisconsin. At the tender age of twenty-two, George and his wife arrived in Castle. Upon his arrival, he tended bar for his brother in January 1888. He eventually bought that saloon from his brother and ran it until the town fizzled out at the turn of the century. George recalled saloon life in 1888 and said there were about seventeen "places" at one time where liquor was sold, but only ten had licenses. The other seven were "houses of virtue." He reminisced, "Crossing Main Street there was a dance hall and saloon that a man from Livingston built and operated. The building was two stories, and the girls roomed over the saloon. They and the girls from the places of easy virtue constituted the female dancers in the dance hall. There was dancing every night, and I think the name of the place was the Badago."

Deadwood, South Dakota, also had its share of dance halls. According to the September 5, 1884, edition of the *Black Hills Daily Times*, a den of prostitution was operating under the guise of a dance hall and was "stocked with unsuspecting and innocent girls." Referring to Albert E. Swearingen's Gem Saloon & Theatre, among those named in the story were: John D. Cornell, Wes. Canagie, Alice Maguire, Maria Marron, Mollie Chappel, Joe Irwin, William L. Dunn, William Pitt Tyler, and Jacob Wertheimer.

Another story from the *Daily* reported, "Swede Johnson, while talking to a respectable lady of Lead, was insulted by one of the *demimonde,* and she immediately interviewed the sidewalk."

In larger towns, prostitutes were more likely to be working as part of a saloon-keeper's organization than on their own. Prostitution and larceny would mingle with liquor and live music in a dangerous, intoxicating evening cocktail. Carl Dupuis recalled just such a scene in Tacoma, Washington: "When I came to Tacoma in 1890 the gambling houses, cheap variety theaters, and honkytonks were still operating wide open and continued to do so for some time afterwards. They were not being run as lawlessly, however, as I had been told they had been in the 1880s. Harry Morgan owned a gambling house, the Comique Theater, and a bar, all connected at South 9th Street and Pacific Avenue about where the Olympus Hotel now stands. In the back rear of his place he had screened booths on a balcony where loggers and sailors were served by jezebels, and they were frequently drugged and robbed of their rolls. It was a tough joint, and the gamblers, bartenders, and bouncers working for Morgan were a vicious lot. Morgan employed a fine band, and he would have it play on a balcony over the theater entrance to attract crowds. He put on good shows in his theater and paid good prices to obtain good acts. John L. Sullivan once gave a sparring exhibition on his stage. Sullivan hung around the place for some time associating with the sporting element and made quite a hit while he was here."

The Wicked West

Bud Brown recalled the Waco Tap in his town, which offered guests carnal pleasures on a remarkably similar system. "The classy saloon of the town was operated by our mayor, G. H. Day, but the notorious place of business was the Waco Tap, a honky-tonk operated by Pony Bell and Dutch Rose. The place was a combination saloon, gambling house, and queen parlor. The place occupied two stories. The ground floor was devoted to the bar, which was about sixty feet long, and a dance floor, and in each of the four corners of the ground floor was some gambling game. The second floor was divided into about 20 rooms, which were occupied by the women who worked in the place. The queens were employed to entertain the men. The girls danced and drank, which was a part of their work. The queens received a percentage of all drinks served to them and their partners. The girls were adept in luring the men into dancing and buying drinks. The ladies would always call for the most expensive drinks, but the bartender would mix the girl's drinks very light so that they could drink and remain sober. The Waco Tap was not the only place of its kind. There were the White Elephant, Occidental, First and Last Chance, and others, which furnished entertainment to the visitors."

Though mostly spoken of in whispers or behind closed doors by more respectable types, sporting girls and their clients often set the fashion standards for their communities. Though the more straitlaced might loathe to admit as much, many envied the prostitutes' access to ready money and a higher degree of haute couture than was often available at the mercantile or general store.

Most women, no matter their location, occupation, or social standing, like to look and smell good. Bathing daily was not a common practice during the Victorian days of the Wild West. However, a daily "toilette" was considered essential. This usually consisted of washing one's face and other delicate areas. The routine, of course, varied depending upon availability of water and products. Men residing in a town or city were also expected to participate in a daily toilette as well. Cowhands and cattle drovers' toilette was more of a "lick and a promise" affair and likely consisted of slapping on a little water from a local stream or watering hole.

The products available in cities and towns for socialites and prostitutes as well included cold cream, perfume, face powder, red rose wash, soap, tooth-whitening powder, hair tonics, and more. Cold cream was used to soften and wash the face, while face powders such as LaBlache and Gossamer were used to give the complexion a smooth finish. In more remote areas, it fell to the woman of the house to make her own cosmetics. One recipe of the 1800s entitled "Cologne for Family Use" calls for:

> ¼ ounce each oils of rosemary and lemon, 1 dram each of bergamot and lavender and cinnamon; 15 drops rose oil, and 2 quarts of common alcohol. Mix and shake from 2 to 3 times a day for a week.

Perfumes were not used as they are today, and were thought to only "cover up" the natural human scent. If used, they were to be used sparingly and in a handkerchief—not on the body. Soft floral or fruit scents were recommended. Musk and Patchouli were considered extremely disagreeable. Some were imported from France and Germany, such as Hoyt's German cologne, while others, such as Floreston and Colgate & Co.'s Cashmere Bouquet, were made in the United States. Lundborg's perfumes from France included fragrances such as

Perfumes were not used as they are today, and were thought to only "cover up" the natural human scent.

Red-light ladies often were at the fashion forefront during non-working hours, and even respectable residents took note of the latest trends.

Alpine Violet, Lily of the Valley, Marechal Nile Rose, and Edenia. Soap varieties included Fisk's Japanese, Kurica, and Pears.

In cities and towns, the clothes worn in the West during the late 1800s often mirrored current fashions worn in most Eastern and Midwestern cities. Just because people were living out West didn't mean they had to wear flour sacks and serapes. Naturally, people living in a rural or remote area would have less to choose from and had looser "dress codes." Most clothes were made in the home, and women bought material from their local dry-goods store. Because they relied on what was delivered, they often had little to work with when making clothes. In the cities, people placed more emphasis on fashion. Fine silks and velvets were readily available, and women made and wore trendier fashions. They also had the option of having their clothes made and custom- fitted for them in millinery and dress shops too. It was thought that to dress well, one needed to have good taste, good sense, and refinement. Even the men dressed appropriately. Yet in true Victorian fashion, women were warned to never let the love of a dress consume her. For love of one's dress was a peril for weak minds.

Types of dress depended upon the time of day and the occasion. For women, by the late 1800s, the glaring colors and loud costumes, once so common, had given way to sober grays, browns, and olives, with black predominating overall. The light, showily trimmed dresses, once worn on the streets as fashionable, were now only worn in carriages. The display of showy dresses and glaring colors was confined to those who felt the need to be ostentatious.

Morning dresses for the street were quite different. This was a more practical ensemble, made of a quiet color and short enough so it did not touch the ground and collect mud and garbage. In winter it was made of woolen goods, while cambric, piqué, Marseilles, or other washable goods were acceptable for summer. Lisle-thread gloves were worn in midsummer, thicker ones in the winter. Linen collars and cuffs were the most suitable for the morning street dress. The bonnet and hat were modest, inexpensive, and matched the dress as closely as possible. During stormy weather, a large waterproof hat was thought to be more convenient and less trouble than an umbrella.

On Sunday, men donned their "morning dress," as wearing evening attire was frowned upon, even in one's one home. The morning dress consisted of a black frock or a black cutaway, a white or black vest (according to the season), gray or colored pants, plaid or stripes (according to the fashion), a high silk or stovepipe hat, and a black scarf or necktie. A black frock coat with black pants was not considered a good combination, nor was a dress coat with colored or light pants. The morning dress was suitable for garden parties, Sundays, social teas, informal calls, morning calls, and receptions.

It was not considered good taste for a man to wear much jewelry—if any at all. They could wear one gold ring, studs, cuff buttons, and a watch chain. However, the watch chain could not be too ostentatious, though it could have a pendant. Anything above that appeared to be a superabundance or ornament.

This is not to say, however, that every man and woman dressed like this in the West. Yes, many did, but there were others, such as cowboys, miners, and prostitutes, who wore clothes that best suited their occupations. Cowboys and miners wore practical work clothes, but more, come Sunday, wore their finery. Prostitutes or red-light ladies, on the other hand, tended to wear a variety of fashions. When working, they wore anything from corsets and undergarments to low-cut dresses. This depended upon where they worked and for whom they worked. However, when they went to shop, they wore the same clothes as the more respectable ladies.

Nevertheless in the West, there existed slaves to fashion, just as we have today. The Grand Hotel bar's proprietor, "Flashy" Jack Allman, for example, was frequently teased about his "trendiness." Jack, who was known to wear new fashions and sport elegant diamond jewelry, now sported a pearl, instead of his diamond. A "millionaire" friend in Paris had written to Jack and told him diamonds were out of fashion and pearls were all the rage. Jack, fashionable man that he was, purchased a magnificent black cat's-eye pearl. He removed his diamond tiepin and replaced it with his new pearl. After a few days of wearing his trendy pearl, he was heard saying it would cost him too much for coal oil to light the Grand Hotel Bar, and it looked so dismal, many persons thought the place was closed for repairs. Fashionable or not, Jack went back to sporting his diamond "headlight."

Chapter 7

Just for Sport

ACROSS THE OLD WEST, DRINKING AND REVELRY led to pranks, tricks, and all kinds of drunken fiascos. Pranks, scams, and general tomfoolery were every bit as entertaining as drinking, whoring, and gambling, and provided a means of entertainment for many, if not all.

The most common tricks were those designed to distract a bartender—and get free drinks. One of them is recorded from the Oriental Saloon. As the story goes, an old tramp of about seventy sat in the back of the saloon near the stove. He slowly worked his way to the bar and said to the barkeep, "Boss, I think I'll go home, but I'd like a drop of the flush come-to-my-face-quick before I go." Since the barkeeper disliked tramps almost as much as he did old men, he obliged, settling on the lesser of the two evils. After the bartender set out the bottle, the old man took a drink so long that it "would paralyze an army mule." He stood at the bar for a few minutes and then made his way to the door.

A few minutes afterward and unbeknownst to the bartender, he returned to the saloon by way of its rear entrance. He took his previous seat by the stove, and after a short time, arose, turned up his collar, and pulled his hat over his eyes. He said to the barkeeper, "Well, I think I'll take a drink and go home; I feel somewhat exhausted from a long walk from Benson." The barkeeper replied, "All right. Pass in your checks, and I'll give you your change." "Well, my boy," said the tramp, "I'm an old man and a poor man and was in hopes you might give me a nightcap." As the barkeeper placed the bottle on the bar, he said, "You look wonderfully like an old tramp I treated a few minutes ago." The old codger replied, "Oh, no, I guess it was my brother." He took his drink and went on his way.

Just moments later the bartender noticed the old tramp back in his seat near the stove, except this time he was wearing an old handkerchief around his neck, his hat tipped to one side, and his coat lapels opened. As he sauntered to the bar for another free drink, the bartender said, "Now look here, my ancient sardine, I'm getting onto your little game, and it won't go. I've treated you twice within the last half an hour." "Oh, no," replied the tramp, "I think it must have been my brother." The barkeeper replied, "Well, just step outside and fetch them all in; I never hurt a man in my life, but I'll be damned if I wouldn't like to start in and make a clean sweep of a whole family." As he reached under the bar for his club, the old vagrant scooted out the door, perhaps to look for his "brother."

> Since so many saloon patrons were armed, alcohol and gunplay were mingled with chilling regularity.

Not every prankster was so harmless. Since so many saloon patrons were armed, alcohol and gunplay were mingled with chilling regularity. Tom J. Snow remembered some of the antics he saw as a bartender in Fort Worth in the 1880s: "Some of the cowhands' favorite sport was to shoot out the lights of an establishment, or start shooting suddenly near a crowd of people. They enjoyed watching the scared folks running away from the shooting. Also, the boys enjoyed fainting

[sic] a gun battle, with someone between them. One night there was a stranger in the bar who had indulged in the cup that cheers slightly too much. He was a sociable fellow and had invited a couple of waddies to join him in taking a drink. The waddies reciprocated by buying a drink, but when it came to pay for their order, they became involved in an argument over which one should do the paying. The waddies didn't waste many words, but started to shoot with the stranger in line of their fire. The stranger attempted to move out from between the two men, but the waddies maneuvered to keep the fellow in the line of fire. There was some fast stepping and dodging for a minute and then, either from exhaustion or an idea, the stranger dropped to the floor. The stranger was as white as an Easter lily and perspiring profusely. The shooting stopped when the stranger dropped to the floor. The scene then changed to the crowd indulging in more refreshments, paid for by the stranger."

As if that weren't bad enough, such marksmanship exhibitions were not uncommon. According to Snow, "Having our lights shot out was an expected event any time a party of waddies arrived at the singing stage."

Fort Worth, Texas, had its share of cowhands in town on a regular basis. They too, enjoyed shooting out the lights. John Raines, a cowhand in Fort Worth in the late 1880s, stated, "My wages were $25, each month with flue lining included, so I had $25 each month for 'baccy and clothes and amusement. For amusement we always rode into Fort Worth, and those days there were plenty of variety in entertainment. Anything one looked for was there, and one could shoot the works. Often, I have seen a bunch of cowhands drive everybody to cover shooting things up. The waddies did the shooting for the fun of seeing folks duck for cover. One night I was with a party of about 15 cowhands, and we were having a good time. We visited a lot of places in the Rush St. district (now Commerce). All were at the point when our hats fit better at the rear of our heads than on the top, which was a sign that most anything could be expected to start popping. We lit into a place, which we always referred to as 14 Rush. A bar, dance hall, gambling, and queens was its combination business. We stood at the pizen bar and then a shot put out a light suddenly. The first shot was followed by others quickly, and all the lights were out before a person had time to figure what was taking place. Soon as the first shot was fired, folks began to run for cover as a bunch of rats scamper for their hole. In the flight, some stumbled over chairs, some over tables, and some over one another. We stepped outside, when all the lights were out on the inside, and some of us shot out the streetlights which were in the district, while others shot in the air. The folks on the street ducked for cover pronto, including two laws. When all the street lights were out in the square and we couldn't see any humans, we mounted hosses and said goodnight to the town. The next day was payoff time for the damage we did, so before the boys parted, a jackpot was made up, which was turned over to Thompson, and he returned the next day to make payment for the lights we destroyed."

Certain drinkers reached the singing stage more often than others, and their musical efforts were not always tolerated. Take Cougar Dick of Granite, Oregon. One pioneer resident there, Mrs. Neil Niven, recalled Dick's unfortunate tendency to burst into song—one song—over and over again: "Cougar Dick *thought* he was the toughest, bravest hombre that ever slapped a poke of dust down on the bar. Cougar Dick not only thought this, but thunderously, boastfully proclaimed it! When that hombre would swagger down the streets, his two guns, hanging loosely in his holsters, slapped and swished against his tightly trousered legs. His jaw was lump shaped by a wad of Star plug that he shifted from one side of his face to the other; a long juicy brown streak aimed with unerring accuracy would attest the transfer.

"When Cougar Dick was drunk he would stand at the bar of the Never Sweat saloon with his buckaroo boot on the brass rail, a glass of whiskey in one hand, and the butt of his gun in the other singing:

Yo! Ho! I'm Cougar Dick, from Gra
Yo! Ho! Yo! Ho! I'm Cougar Dick, an
Yo! Yo! Ho! Cause Cougar Dick from ᴄ
    trump your trick!
Yo! Ho! Yo! Ho! I'm Cougar Dick!"

Mrs Niven went on to explain: "We people of Granite
to most every odd quirk a man could have, but Cougar Dick s.
our quality of mercy. To call the bluff of our yo-ho-ing friend, the ɪ
of the town staged an elaborate but effective joke. A dummy, made oɪ
straw and dressed in typical miner's garb, was placed on the rocks at
the base of a high cliff at the entrance of Gruel's gulch. At the crest of
the cliff, several men waited with rifles. The others then went back to
the Never Sweat saloon where Cougar Dick had struck his usual
stance and was lustily vouching for his virility. The men sat down and
listened to his boastful song. Soon Cougar Dick was interrupted by a
man running into the saloon and excitedly yelling, 'Come on fellows,
somebody has been murdered down at Gruel's gulch!' In just a
moment, the saloon was emptied.

"When the men were close enough to the cliff to distinguish the
dummy body from the rocks, the men on the crest of the cliff started
firing a volley of shots. Bullets fell all around the men, who rapidly
searched for places of safety. Shortly the firing ceased and a loud voice
boomed out, 'We're gonna lead up Cougar Dick next!' Well, yo, ho,
our Cougar Dick from Granite Creek crawled away from the men on
his belly, sneaking quite a ways down the road. Suddenly he jumped
to his feet and started running hell-bent for Sumpter. The men who
were not doubled-up laughing fired a few shots at the rapidly retreat-
ing figure. Grant Thornburg, sheriff at Sumpter, knew of the joke.
When Cougar Dick arrived, Thornburg arranged for a salesman to
take the same train out as Cougar Dick, to follow him suspiciously
as if he were out to lead him up. All the way to Baker the salesman

ed the frightened Cougar Dick. Every time he moved the sales-
followed him, looking as menacing as possible. The moment the
in pulled in at Baker, Cougar Dick jumped off and ran to catch
nother one. We never heard of him again. Afterwards for many
years, whenever a man showed a little streak of yellow, they would
say he had 'Cougar Dick courage.'"

While towns in the Old West had to contend with rough crowds
and tough hombres, whether they be cowhands or miners, they did
not have to tolerate the single obnoxious ones. While it may not have
been so easy for townsfolk to deal with a group of ruffians, it was easier to mount an attack or shame against one offender—Cougar Dick
is a prime example. By doing this, the townspeople not only removed
a blight from their community, but they united as a group for a common purpose.

In addition to private jokes and pranks, the Old West also saw its
share of public sport. Boxing was very popular at the time, and
famous boxers of the day toured the country to hosts of delighted
fans. Mark Twain wrote a letter to Olivia Clemens regarding his take
on professional boxing: "A round consists of only 3 minutes; then the
men retire to their corners and sit down and lean their heads back
against a post and gasp and pant like fishes, while one man fans them
with a fan, another with a tablecloth, another rubs their legs and
sponges off their faces and shoulders and blows sprays of water in
their faces from his own mouth. Only one minute is allowed for this;
then time is called and they jump up and go to fighting again. It is
absorbingly interesting."

The Marquis of Queensbury Rules brought uniform regulations
to the sport of boxing. Prior to then, men fought bare-knuckled. The
rules were written and put into practice in the 1860s, though it wasn't
until 1892 that the first official heavyweight-title boxing match
fought with gloves and under the rules of the Marquis of Queensbury
took place. That match ended when James J. Corbett, the famous

⇨ MARQUIS OF QUEENSBURY BOXING RULES ⇦

The Marquis of Queensbury Rules were the regulations under which most fights were held. The Republican *newspaper, published in Tombstone, Arizona Territory, wrote:*

Most of the recent contests between noted pugilists have been governed by what are known as the Marquis of Queensbury Rules. To most persons these rules are an enigma. To such the *Republican* presents them in full, with the statement that they were furnished by the noted authority in sporting matters, Richard K. Fox, of the *Police Gazette*:

Rule #1. The fight has to be a fair stand-up boxing match, in a 24-foot ring, or as near that size as practicable.

Rule #2. No wrestling or hugging allowed. The rounds to be of three or four minutes' duration, and one minute rest time.

Rule #3. If either man falls through weakness or otherwise, he must get up unassisted, ten seconds to be allowed him to do so, the other meanwhile retire to his corner, and when the fallen man is on his legs the round is to be resumed and continued until the three minutes have expired, and if one man fails to come to the scratch in the ten seconds allowed, it shall be in the power of the referee to give us his award in favor of the other man.

Rule #4. A man hanging on the rope in a helpless state, with his toes off the ground, shall be considered down. No seconds or any other person to be allowed in the ring during the rounds.

Rule #5. Should the contest be stopped by any unavoidable interference, the referee to name time and place for finishing the contest as soon as possible, so that the match must be won or lost, unless the backers of both men agree to draw their stakes

Rule #6. The gloves to be fair-sized boxing gloves of the best quality, and new.

Rule #7. Should a glove burst or come off, it must be replaced to the referee's satisfaction.

Rule #8. A man on one knee is considered down, and if struck is entitled to the stakes.

Rule #9. No shoes or boots with spikes allowed.

"Gentleman Jim," knocked out reigning champ John L. Sullivan in the twenty-first round. Corbett lost his title to Robert Fitzsimmons in 1897.

By the late 1800s, professional boxing matches, which usually meant a trophy or medal was at stake, had become quite formal. In 1883, Neil McLeod and James Young, both of Tombstone, met one evening, not to box, but to sign legal papers. The papers were articles drawn up so the men could fight for the Police Gazette Championship. The articles stated the two men were competing for the Police Gazette champion medal of Arizona and must fight according to the Police Gazette's rules. The match was supposed to be held at Schieffelin Hall on September 22 between 7 and 10 p.m., but McLeod came down with bilious fever, and the match was postponed. The fight was eventually held in early October, and after four short rounds, Young was taken out, and McLeod took the $400 purse.

Prizefighter Neil McLeod was supposed to step into the ring again to fight for his title in early 1884, but because of a discrepancy in the rules it was postponed. His opponent, Frank White, insisted the fight be held under the London Prizefighter rules, while McLeod wanted to fight under the Marquis of Queensbury rules or the Police Gazette rules. White wanted to fight under the London rules, because he could win the title after just one match. Under the other rules, a fighter had to win three times to earn his title.

Men like McLeod and Young were well known in their day, especially in regional circles, but are now largely forgotten. Prizefighters all over the West completed in regional competitions, but it wasn't until the 1890s that boxers attained real celebrity status.

Wrestling, especially Greco-Roman style, was another popular sport with devoted fans in many areas. The late 1880s and 1890s gave rise to a passion for exercise and physical fitness among Victorians, and wrestling was related to that craze. Many matches took place, and the winner earned a cash prize.

JUST FOR SPORT

On February 9, 1884, a Greco-Roman wrestling match was held between "Professor" Ed Wilson and former newspaperman Richard Rule. Wilson, a regular at Tombstone's new gymnasium, and Rule met to discuss the conditions of the match. They agreed the match should be held publicly at Schieffelin Hall; the winner would net $250. Both men began their training; Wilson started his day with several miles of mountain climbing, several hours of club swinging, exercising on the horizontal bars, and other muscle-developing activities. Rule, on the other hand, was said to have awakened early, walked to the Pick-'em Up and back, which was halfway to Charleston, and during leisure hours, wrestled with prizefighter Neil McLeod.

Both men appeared on the night of the match and gave the crowd its money's worth. The hall was packed. Even some of Tombstone's female citizens were seen sitting on the stage. At 8:49 p.m. the men met in the center and shook hands. While both men were said to be in fine physical shape, each had a different physique. Rule was described as symmetrical with a graceful build, while Wilson was said to be of massive strength. In action, the men were different as well, Rule being very quick and active, while Wilson was slower in his movements.

The *Epitaph* wrote, "Suffice it to say Rule displayed a knowledge of the science of Greco-Roman wrestling that was a surprise to all and particularly gratifying to his friends. The first fall was scored by Wilson in twenty-one minutes ... his opponent made wary by experience, put himself entirely on the defensive, and by resorting to the devices known to wrestlers, exhausted the time without losing another fall, therefore winning the match, the conditions being that Wilson was to throw Rule twice in an hour, or lose. The exhibition was conducted throughout in a manner to meet approval of the audience, which at the close greeted the victor with much applause." When Rule married Edith Anderson in 1887, the *Epitaph* wrote that it hoped "that the little Rules may not transgress the big Rules. It's a poor Rule that doesn't work both ways."

The Wicked West

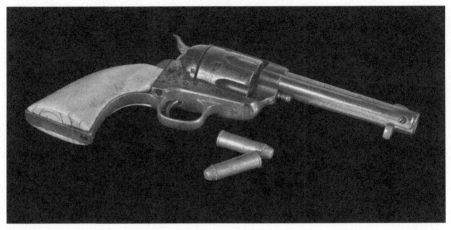

A rare 1880 single-action Colt Revolver with a handle fashioned from a single piece of ivory. (Objects courtesy of Tombstone Western Heritage Museum.)

Healthy exercise and spectator sport aside, by far the most popular remained the sport of some good old-fashioned fighting and shooting. Fighting and shooting seemingly went hand in hand in the Old West. Too much drink, an angry temper, and firearms were a bad mix. Even though most towns had restrictions on carrying weapons in town, it sometimes didn't seem to matter. Local town folk didn't take kindly to it either, but they knew that if the town was to survive and make money, they had to endure the occasional gambler and cowboy kicking up their heels.

Shootings took place in just about every Western city, and variety theaters and saloons saw their share of them, though it did little to deter fortune-seekers. In a place where gunslingers were everywhere, firearms were very much a part of daily life. Frank Heiner, an old Montanan, recalled the wild scene at Fort Brenton, where "the saloons were full all the time. There were shootin' scrapes every day, but that didn't make no difference in the population." The Park Theatre in Tucson was another one of those places. According to pioneer resident C. C. Wheeler, "Tucson at this point [early 1880s] was full of rough characters who had drifted in when the railroad was completed to this point and several shooting affrays took place but only one killing took place. These would usually happen over some of the women, while others would be by some bad 'hombre full of whiskey' who would show off by shooting a bottle off the bar or at the lights."

Most establishments learned to live with a certain level of violence, and some of them seemed to be almost built for it. Mr. Joe Prewitt arrived in Durango, Colorado, in 1861, and in May 1882 he moved to nearby Farmington, New Mexico. At that time Farmington contained only about ten buildings, all of them made of adobe, with dirt roofs. "Not a shingle in the town." "Well," he said, "it was just as well, and in some instances, better; for frequently, there would be a group of cowboys sitting in a saloon, and just for amusement, they would shoot through the roof with their six-shooters, which would have made a regular sieve of a singled roof, but with a dirt roof it did but little harm, for the bullet could be seen to raise a little streak of dirt a few inches in the air, then the dirt in the roof would just settle back and the hole closed up."

Experienced saloon owners learned to watch for the danger signs when a jovial cowboy might suddenly start terrorizing other customers. William (Billy) Blevins, a saloon owner in Colorado City, Texas, remembered learning the business in the young town of Toyah. "I put up a saloon building, it was just thrown together, but it served my purpose. I had a good size bar in front and a pool and billiard table in the rear. The style those days was to decorate the back bar with fancy colored glasses by pyramiding them at different parts. I soon learned to discard the attractive glasses. The cowhands would come in and get a drink. With the first drink he would push his hat back a little, with the next one, his hat would go back a little further and so on until that hat was setting on the back part of the fellow's head. Then the cowhand was ready for some kind of action. Those pretty glasses I had on the back bar always drew the attention of the man with his hat setting at the back of his head. If there were several together they would have a shooting match using the fancy glasses as their target. Of course they would hit the glasses and continue the game until the targets were all gone, or become tired of the sport and turn their attention to something else. Perhaps it would be the billiard balls they would decide to shoot off the table. They may stop with the billiard balls or turn to the light and shoot those. I never questioned them about their shooting."

Blevins learned not only when a customer was about to turn into a shooting hazard, but also, ironically, to trust the man about to pull a gun in the middle of a bar. According to Blevins, "When one of them sprees were pulled by a bunch of cowhands, I knew that the next day they would be back and pay for the damage to my furniture that they did. They never failed to do such with me. The real cowhand was a square man. I moved to Colorado City after staying in Toyah for two years. I run a saloon there for eight years; it was the cow center of that section. During my eight years there I had no trouble. I used the same system I used in Toyah.... They resorted to the same kind of tricks to amuse themselves."

In some towns, such wild behavior was actually a rite of passage. A former Marlin, Texas, resident, Mrs. Emma Falconer, recalled that "A special stunt of the cowboys was to ride into the saloon and shoot a barrel of whiskey until they could take a glass and catch their drink, then ride away and the next day return and tell the owner to put his price on the damage. This has happened here in Marlin and some of the oldest families boys have been among the number, but who, as they grew to manhood made law-abiding citizens."

Other saloon owners coped with the uncertainty by channeling their customers' destructive energy into more organized fights. Mr. Earl Heath, a newcomer to the town of Prague, Oklahoma, described the saloon scene there at the turn of the century as if it were something out of the Chuck Pahlaniuk novel *Fight Club*. "When the railroad was built through Prague, work gangs of fifty to seventy-five men would come to town when they had been paid. It meant good business for the local saloon. The bartender would set 'em up to the whole gang. Then he would point to two big fellows of his picking and say, 'You and you.' This meant the exhibition of the free-for-all fight for the amusement of the whole gang. When the fight was over and the crowd had laughed it off between drinks, the keeper would repeat, 'you and you,' picking another pair to fight for the amusement of the crowd. The drinking and social fighting would continue throughout the night, when toward morning, the gang would depart in pairs for their bunks at the railroad construction quarters."

Tombstone, Arizona, was a wealthy town filled with miners, gamblers, cowboys, and businessmen. But like most towns, there was tension amongst a select few. In one corner there was the county sheriff John Behan and his cowboys, and on the other side you had the city marshal Virgil Earp and his brothers. The town citizens were split down the middle. As tensions grew over politics, romance, and money, so did tempers.

An incident in October 1880 between gambler John "Doc" Holliday, who sided with Virgil Earp, and saloon owner Milton Joyce, who was against Virgil Earp, was likely part of the town's growing feud. It seems Johnny Tyler and Doc Holliday had been in a shooting scrape earlier that evening, but were separated and disarmed by mutual friends before anything serious happened. Joyce asked Tyler to leave the saloon, so he did. Holliday was also asked to leave, but refused. Joyce also "remonstrated" Holliday for creating a disturbance in the saloon. Deciding to leave, Holliday went to the bar and asked for his gun. He was refused his pistol, so he angrily left. Shortly thereafter, he returned with a "self-cocker." He spoke some words to Joyce and then fired his gun at him. Joyce, no more than ten feet away, jumped at Holliday and knocked him on the head with a six-shooter. However, before Joyce could stop him, Holliday managed to fire twice. The first shot hit Joyce in the hand, and the other struck Joyce's partner, Mr. Parker, in his big toe. Joyce was taken out of the saloon, and Holliday was placed in a chair in the saloon. Because of Holliday's bloody appearance, those on hand thought his wounds severe, if not fatal. Seeing Holliday's wounds were not that serious, Deputy Marshal Earp arrested him. He was charged with assault with a deadly weapon and intent to kill. Judge Reilly set his bail for $200, which he promptly furnished.

Incidents like these led up to the gunfight that took place on October 26, 1881, behind the O. K. Corral between the Earps and the cowboys. Tombstone chronicler Clara Brown described the incident: "The inmates of every house in town were greatly startled by the sudden report of firearms, about 3 p.m., discharged with such lightning-like rapidity that it could be compared only to the explosion of a bunch of firecrackers; and the aspect of affairs grew more portentous when, a few moments later, the whistles of the steam hoisting works sounded a shrill alarm. 'The cowboys!' cried some, thinking that a party of those desperadoes were 'taking the town.' 'The Indians,' cried a few of the most excitable. Then, after it was learned that a fight had been engaged in between Marshal Earp, his two brothers, a special deputy (Doc Holliday), and four cowboys ... speculation as to the cause of the affray ran riot. In the midst of this, when the scene upon the streets was one of intense excitement, the whistle again sounded, and directly well-armed citizens appeared from all quarters, prepared for any emergency. This revealed what was not before generally known—the existence of a 'Vigilance Committee,' composed of law-abiding citizens who organized with the determination of upholding right and combating wrong, and who agreed upon a signal of action from the mines. Their services were not needed, however, on this occasion."

A writer for *Harper's New Monthly Magazine* arrived in town in the midst of the hearing. He wrote, "The Grand Jury was now in session and hearing the evidence in the case. It was rumored that the town party, as the Earps were called, would be able to command sufficient influence to go free of indictment. The country cowboys, on the other hand, were flocking into town, and on one quiet Sunday in particular, things wore an ominous look. It was said that should justice fail to be done, the revengeful, resolute looking men conferring together darkly at the edges of the sidewalk together would attempt to take the matter into their own hands."

According to Judge Spicer, who presided over the hearing, Virgil Earp, as chief of police, and Morgan and Wyatt Earp, and Doc Holliday, whom he called upon for help, went to the site of the fight, near the O. K. Corral, for the purpose of arresting and disarming the Clantons and McLaurys. He did feel there was enough evidence to support a trial.

Towns all over the West had disputes like this; albeit few garnered this much attention. San Angelo, Texas, was the site of a gun battle between some cowhands and gamblers. Gaston Fergenson, a lifelong resident at the time, recalled the event: "A gambler attempted to cheat a waddy and got caught in the act. When the waddy demanded his money, the gambler refused to turn it over. The waddy drew his gun and so did the gambler. Shots were exchanged, and the waddy was wounded. Other waddies took up the fight for their pal, and other gamblers took up the fight for their pal, and a battle took place. The cowhands went gunning for gamblers. There was lots of shooting. Several men were wounded. One waddy and two gamblers were killed. The fight ended when there were no more gamblers in sight to shoot at. All the gamblers went into hiding. The cowhands rode from one place to another and would ride into the joints. They shot at every gambler in sight and put the lights out with bullets. When the waddies quit the town, it was well cleaned. The San Angelo waddy-gambler fight was one of the worst battles I ever saw in a town, but gun battles were not unusual in those days."

Sometimes the feuds were professional, as was the case between the cowhands and the gamblers, but sometimes, the battles were the result of differences in race and culture. As Mrs. Neil Niven, of Granite, Oregon, said in the late 1800s: "Usually when someone got liquored up he would march up and down the streets shooting off his guns. One source of amusement for him was getting the Chinese separated from one another, then making one of them do the bullet dance. This was accomplished by one or several men firing at the luckless creature's feet, and he had to jump and dance to keep from getting hit. I don't ever remember anyone being hurt by this odd amusement, but most likely there was. We girls use to wish sometimes that the Chinese would get a hold of a white man and make him dance to the tune of their knives. All of the Orientals packed knives for protection, but they only used them among themselves and not that very often."

Chapter 8

The Temperance Wars

A BRAHAM LINCOLN ONCE SAID, "It has been my experience that folks who have no vices have very few virtues." While
Lincoln may have thought a few vices were okay, not everyone
in the West thought drinking, smoking, and gambling were acceptable.
Some truly believed they were vices of the devil himself. As the towns,
cities, and settlements of the Old West became more civilized, the pen-
dulum of popular opinion swung away from tolerance of its wilder
aspects and more toward reform. Women were highly influential in
this area, and the Temperance movement was intimately linked to an
increased awareness and push for women's rights. After all, supporting
a houseful of kids with an unpredictable income meant most females
had little patience for their men's indulgence in booze, brawls, and
gambling.

The U.S. Census statistics surrounding malt liquors showed that
in 1880, there were 2,191 drinking establishments, which employed
26,220 people. *Harper's Monthly* magazine reported that while the
growth of production and consumption of malt liquors was note-
worthy, the average consumption was not more than eleven barrels
per head per year. Employees in most U.S. breweries at the time
received perquisites in the form of about as much beer as they could
drink. Some breweries even offered employees brass checks for

Frustrated with wayward husbands, violence, and the high costs of the high life, women took matters into their own hands.

twenty glasses of beer at the beginning of their shift. A brass check was a coin made of brass, usually stamped with goods printed on them. The *Harper's* magazine stated, "It is claimed that insanity arising from intemperance is significantly less where beer is drunk, and that consumption of malt and of distilled liquors is in inverse ratio in the several countries, so that the more beer, the less spirits."

In contrast to the census statistics, an 1880 book entitled *Stimulants & Narcotics* simply stated that "the wide use of felicity-producing drugs is one of the most stupendous evils which afflict humanity. The alcohol habit is unquestionably one of the greatest of all blights which affect our modern civilization. The popular notion that it is a stimulant has given rise to its use not only as a beverage, but as a common remedy for disease, and with most disastrous effects." Several different writers published books like this one to combat the wanton ways Americans lived in the 1880s, and their works found a ready audience among housewives, clergy, teachers, and reformers.

Stimulants and Narcotics went on to tackle the so-called medical and scientific, moral, psychological, and economic arguments in favor of the use of alcohol, arguing passionately against it:

> Thousands of editors, lawyers, students, authors, and even clergymen, keep beside their midnight lamps a bottle of wine or brandy, and consider one as indispensable as the other. They imagine that with the frequent drams they quaff from that green bottle, they imbibe an increase of mental vigor.
>
> .   .   .
>
> The moderate drinker takes his morning dram to fortify his stomach for the reception of his breakfast. Immediately after breakfast he must have another glass to assist digestion. But how does alcohol assist digestion? Not by dissolving the food, for its effect is to harden tissues. This, then, is a monstrous fallacy.

Especially compelling are the author's arguments against the "moral" or biblical justifications for the use of wine:

> At the present time there is a powerful party who claim that the use of fermented or intoxicating liquors is permitted and even sanctioned by the Bible. This party is headed by a few eminent scholars and clergymen, who are chiefly supported by a promiscuous throng of rich rum sellers, respectable moderate drinkers, and gutter drunkards. The Bible has been quoted to sustain polygamy, slavery, and other evil institutions, as well as intemperance. Rightly understood, it supports none of these evils.

Attempts to tar drinkers with a moral and religious brush eventually escalated to the point where alcohol itself became the culprit.

The Wicked West

As with any public relations campaign, zealous advocates in the movement eventually discovered that it was far less effective to deride the drinkers as morally weak than it was to personify drink itself as "evil." Or, as the book goes on to state: "Alcohol is the horrid fiend we are fighting, no matter under what guise it comes."

This zealous advocacy against alcohol even spilled over into other beverages. Another section in the book describes how tea and coffee encouraged drunkenness. It reads, "this statement will doubtless startle those who have been taught to believe that there is no evil in 'the cup that cheers and not inebriates' but we are prepared to show that the influence of the use of these poisons (for such they are) directly tends to encourage drinking stronger stimulants, though our present space will not allow us to enter into a discussion of that subject."

It also stated, "Tobacco using and drunkenness go hand in hand. Nearly, if not quite, every drunkard chews or smokes. The great majority of drunkards became addicted to the use of tobacco first. Thus they learned to demand a stimulus of some kind. The feverish heat produced by tobacco required quenching, and liquor was resorted to. Either is bad enough alone; but rum and tobacco together are blasting the human race like a simoon from the heart of hell."

Another person who felt that drinking, smoking, and gambling was the devil's work was Reverend William Hill, who paid a visit to Tombstone, Arizona, in 1880. According to his first report to Bishop J. F. Spalding of the Episcopal Church of Los Angeles, "The town or city of Tombstone now numbers two thousand inhabitants, and it is rapidly growing. Those interested believe that it will be another Virginia City, and, although they may be too sanguine, no one can doubt but that it will be a large and growing place …. It should be supplied with services as soon as possible."

In his second letter to the Bishop he wrote, "I will try and give you as a correct an impression of Tombstone as is in my power, seeking neither to give a more rosy hue or darker color than present facts and future prospects warranted." In the reverend's report, he noted Tombstone's appearance and compared it to California mining towns twenty-five years past, with its sprawling features. For a man of the cloth, the moral life in Tombstone must have been rather shocking: "There is the same mushroom appearance of the buildings, the same reckless characters, making day and night hideous. The same almost unlimited gambling and drinking; the same absence of families, and the same disregard for God's holy day; I suppose there are at least sixty places of business there, and I could hear of but *two* that closed their doors for an hour on Sunday. Here too, the strange woman whose steps take hold on hell, plies her woeful trade, and many are her victims who should live a sober, righteous, and godly life." He also reported, "With families will

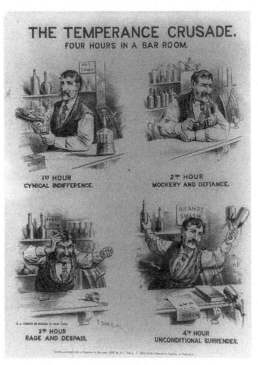

The perils of drink and "demon rum."

come social elevation and a desire for Church privileges and then the change will be like magic.... I will keep an eye on Tombstone."

Mark Twain also had some thoughts on the subject: "How I do hate those enemies of the human race who go around enslaving God's free people with pledges—to quit drinking instead of to quit wanting to drink."

One Fort Worth saloon owner made a more practical effort to "save" the good people of his town. Pioneer resident Andre Jorgensen Anderson wrote: "Those days certain people of the town would take a spasm of righteousness and demand that gambling be stopped on the Sabbath day. Occasionally, the officials would concede a point and send forth an order to stop gambling on the Sabbath day and to close all places where gambling was operated. Such orders would hold forth until the spasm cooled, which generally took three or four weeks. Low had his gambling apparatus arranged so he could move it easily. Therefore, when an order would be received to close all gambling places on the Sabbath day, Mr. Low moved his gambling paraphernalia out of his establishment and continued to operate the rest of his business on the Sabbath. This act of Low caused vehement protest, but the officials were of the opinion that when the gambling paraphernalia was moved out of the establishment, it ceased to be a gambling house. Monday morning gambling resumed."

For some towns and some men, alcohol was more than an occasional nuisance or a moral smirch—it was a very dangerous drug.

For some towns and some men, alcohol was more than an occasional nuisance or a moral smirch—it was a very dangerous drug. In places like Soda Springs, Idaho, the arrival of a railroad could bring on a flood of humanity. Many citizens saw their civic dreams ruined by sleazy saloons and lowlifes just traveling through.

Soda Springs was transformed by the railroad reaching it, much to the dismay of some. In 1881 it was a quiet little hamlet. There was scarcely a noise heard louder than the bubbling of the health-giving springs. However, once the railroad reached it around August 1882, all that changed. Basic food prices and provisions rose nearly 100 percent in value. The only cheap commodity was whiskey. A resident at the time wrote, "I look from my window upon half a dozen saloons. At night, I sleep with a pistol under my pillow and a double barrel shotgun by my side, kept awake by the shrieks and howls of drunken men. These wretched bummers, who have come here to build up the town have torn down or defaced the spring houses, defiled the waters, and for the present, at least, made a place almost uninhabitable. Shooting in the saloons is of such common occurrence that it is little noticed, but horse stealing is a crime that seldom goes without speedy punishment if the thieves can be caught."

For some, saloons and drinking offered the possibility of a life without employment, or at least minimal work. Superior, Montana, also had its share of saloon and drinking rowdiness. Mrs. Lizzie (Sarah E.) Miles came to Superior from Kansas in 1891 and recalled a man in town who appeared to never actually purchase his cigars. She remembered, "That was the year Superior was moved to its present site. There were just three or four homes, but seven saloons. Most of the miners at the dance drank up pretty freely, and before the night was over, they'd all be singing and having a gay time. 'There'll Be a Hot Time in the Old Town To-Night,' was the most popular tune, and usually it was a hot time. Murray, 'the Roller,' was more like a shaggy dog than a man, what with his whiskers and long hair hanging down his shoulders. He asked if he could camp on our place, when we were in the Jimmy Harmon cabin west of town; he didn't do us any harm, so we let him. He rolled two big logs under a big tree, and slept between them. He was followed around by a ring-necked dog he called Bob. When he couldn't bum a quarter off anybody, he'd live on lamb's quarter greens, eating them like spare grass. He never bothered us at the ranch, and used to buy a quart of milk, whenever he could steal a dime to pay for it."

The Wicked West

Fellow resident Irene Bundrick remembered Murray. "I remember clearly, Murray, 'the Roller'; I don't know that I ever heard his exact name. He had long hair, which he usually twisted into a knot covered by his hat. He was well educated, and when sober, was much in demand among the miners as a letter-writer. He lived in a long log cabin, just south and west of the bridge crossing the Missoula River, a few feet north of where the Strand Theatre now stands. A professional bum, sleeping with the pigs in his drunkenness, he could juggle the King's English."

Just as the Old West inspired wild drinking, crazed gambling, and all sorts of impassioned stunts, religious organizations rose to the challenge of preaching to very rambunctious flocks. Preachers had to compete with saloons, bordellos, casinos, boxing matches, and the potential riches of mining for their congregations' attentions. Many of them decided to confront the competition head-on.

"Lips that touch liquor..." was the war cry of many members of the Temperance movement.

Mrs. Ernest P. Truesdell was a pioneer resident of Canyon City, Oregon, and she recalled life there near the turn of the century. She said, "A wild, and woolly, rollicking mining camp is the best way I can describe Canyon City when I first came here. The men could throw a ball in the air, draw, shoot, and take a drink of whiskey before the ball would hit the ground. The women packed a Bible in one hand and, figuratively speaking, a teamster's whip in the other. The early Methodist revival meetings, were noted for their boisterousness. The preachers that came to town always stirred up plenty of Hell-fear and Hell-raising. Saloons and their attendant evils gave cause for real work for the revivalists. They would curse and revile the saloon element at every meeting."

According to Truesdell, the religious message went out first to women in a community, who then passed it on to their families. "At a series of meetings, we had a tall, stately, dynamic, southern revivalist leading the congregation into less sinful paths. His silver tongue could tell the saloon element they were heading for Hell in more ways than you would think possible. The women would hear the tales of Hell-fire, and pack them home and unload on their less active religious husbands. It was a standing joke that everybody stayed up an hour later during the nights the revivalist was in town, so the wives could rail at their husbands."

At one of these sermons, Truesdell recalled that the preacher did not meet with as much success as usual. "The 'Stench of Hell' sermon, as it was later called, started off with its usual dynamic criticism of the saloon. As the preacher reviled the saloons he noticed a slackening of interest, as if there was something diverting the congregation's attentions. He talked louder and more vociferously against whiskey—but still they wiggled and squirmed. Never stopping his flow of vituperation, he slowly stalked up the aisle towards the stove to see what was the matter. When he got about halfway there he suddenly stopped talking and his face became contorted with rage and revulsion. Someone of the saloon element had rubbed Limburger cheese on the stove and the benches near the stove. The heat from the stove, melting the cheese, made an unbearable stench. In fact it was a smell that surely 'smelled to heaven,' and we had to go home."

The scientific evidence promoted by temperance advocates was often as dubious as the theories coming from the other side. While one popular medical opinion insisted that drinking was healthful because alcohol preserved (or pickled) the tissues of the body, many temperance advocates sincerely believed that excessive alcohol consumption was the leading cause of human spontaneous combustion.

Others insisted alcohol was not found in living organisms, but only in decaying vegetable matter as a result of fermentation—hence its link with death and decay.

For all the debate and all the politicking that ensued over sin and reform, however, few took into account the role vice played in the economics of building the frontier. Saloons sprang up in every town not because Americans were alcoholics or addicted gamblers, but because the heady mix of entertainments offered there proved to be very good business and afforded otherwise isolated and overworked people a chance for necessary socializing. Rich and poor could rub shoulders at the saloon. One man might order a shot of cheap whiskey, and another might spend thousands on fancy cocktails and games of chance. As social institutions, saloons were easily adaptable to new demands—as a town expanded and gentrified, new fittings and fancy liquors might replace the staple beer and whiskey. Since saloons fulfilled a need for a social gathering place in a frontier culture that didn't have much use for rules and expectations, their business boomed. And when the saloon business boomed, other businesses were not far behind.

Fort Worth's Andre Jorgenson Anderson saw the trend clearly in his adopted hometown. "It is a fact, the saloon, gambling houses, and queen houses were one of the chief factors contributing to building Fort Worth. The natural human desire for diversion and entertainment caused these men to seek it when they had time off from their work. The town, which presented the best variety of entertainment that these men desired, was the town to which they would go. These men lived a rough life and enjoyed rough amusement. They gambled with their life every day while at work. Therefore, many of them also obtained a thrill gambling for money. The human being, by nature, is a social being and desires company. Men enjoy mixing with his fellow man and engaging in social activities. The cowboy was not interested in pink teas, ping pong, or any other entertainment of that nature."

Across the West, towns catered to such men. Without their business, it was difficult to keep the economy of a small frontier settlement functioning. The more successful a community was at entertaining visitors, the better it would be at attracting trade and investment, and the more likely that it would become better known as a good place to spend the evening or strike a deal. That's certainly how things worked in Anderson's town.

To business-minded Westerners, saloon-owning was a path to fortune. Bud Brown of Fort Worth followed his father's example, tending bar in his old man's saloon before going into business himself in Colorado City. "My father ... chose the saloon business because it was one of the leading lines and doing the greatest business of all other lines, during that period .... It was a typical frontier cow town and the town's sole support came from cattlemen. There was an abundance of money. It was not unusual to see a man reach in his pocket and pull out a pouch containing several hundred dollars in $20-gold coins."

> The cowboy was not interested in pink teas, ping pong, or any other entertainment of that nature.

Brown didn't live to regret his decision. He recalled one convention in Colorado City in 1886 that netted him large profits: "The meeting was attended by all the leading ranchers of the district, and many came from distant places. To say that the town was busy waiting on the trade is stating the situation mildly. There existed a scramble on the part of the visitors to get waited on. My bar was crowded from the hour of opening till we closed in the wee hours of the morning. Rancher after rancher would come in and call every person in the bar up to 'name their pizen.' When a rancher gave such order, each bartender would report to me the total charge for the drinks he served. I then would total the bill for the treater, who would place the money, usually in gold coins, on the bar. The amounts were from $5 to $15, and many times more, especially if champagne had been served. Such treats as I have described were not just an occasional happening, but frequent during the convention."

Chapter 9

The Long Arm of the Law

A S THEY BECAME MORE PROFITABLE, saloons began to attract a degree of official attention that had less to do with progressive reform movements, religion, and regulations for the public health than it had to do with money. Thus it was no accident that one of the most effective, and rewarding, forms of control was to use licensing fees, taxes, and permits to control the activities that saloons offered. In some towns, the regulation of liquor and gambling occupied center stage in political discourse.

For example, Virginia City, Nevada, was home to one of the largest silver strikes in U.S. history. In 1859, silver was discovered, and people raced to get there. By 1862, Virginia City had a population of close to 3,000. Close to its peak in 1875, this "bonanza" town was home to nearly 20,000 people. After the organization of the Territory of Nevada, the charter of Virginia City was amended to conform more nearly to the habits and customs of the citizens. Section 8 granted powers to the trustees; the words "and providing for licensing bars at which spirituous liquors are sold" were underlined. The board of trustees was also given power to levy and provide for the collections of license tax on all billiard tables and nine ten-pin alleys kept for public use. In 1881, Myron Angel's *History of the State of Nevada* stated: "The authorities of Utah never encourage the sale of liquors,

The Wicked West

By 1888, Helena, Montana, would be home to some fifty millionaires.

never permit it if possible to prevent it. Of course this was an impossibility from the very commencement with such a population as made up Virginia City. 'Whiskey or death' would have been a rallying cry to rouse the whole population."

Local governments usually weren't the only political body trying to tap into the wealthy saloons. Believe it or not, saloon, tobacco, and similar business owners had to deal with Internal Revenue collectors. Internal Revenue required each to have a license, whether it was for a brewery, a saloon, or the sale of tobacco. The licenses were annual, but needed to be punched for each month they were used. Each town was assigned a revenue officer. He was supplied with the necessary blank forms, and business owners were urged to get their forms as soon as possible to avoid severe penalties.

One of the best-documented boomtowns of the West, Tombstone, also happened to be a place that was very particular about its licenses. One September, the city council members amended ordinance number four, which provided for the licensing of any business or trade being conducted within the city limits. It was a misdemeanor not to have a license, and guilty parties were fined up to $100 or imprisoned for a maximum of thirty days, or both. The monthly licensing fees were as follows:

Assayers	$ 1.50	
Billiard Tables	1.50	(per table)
Breweries	4.00	

Circus or Menagerie	12.50	(per day, while in town)
Club Rooms	7.00	(where cards and dice were played for drinks)
Hotels (first-class)	6.00	(twenty bed maximum)
Ice	4.00	(selling or delivering)
Pawnbrokers	10.00	(must keep detailed record books)
Ten-Pin Alleys	4.00	(per alley)

Some of the other licensing fees were a bit more complicated. Liquor licenses cost $2 per day or $60 per month at the discretion of the owner. The ordinance read, "The owners or lessee of any house, room, or cellar, where wines, malt, or spirituous liquors are sold by the bottle or glass, where dancing is carried on and generally known as dance houses or cellars shall pay ...."

The license for barrooms matched that of a liquor license, except it applied to every person or firm engaged in keeping a barroom or public saloon. The cost of the license varied depending on the bar's monthly receipts. A first-class license applied to those whose sales were $800 or higher and cost $7 per month. The monthly fees for second- and third-class licenses varied, depending upon the sales.

Gambling licenses were even more complex. The ordinance read, "For each and every person who shall deal, play, or carry on, open, or cause to be opened, or who shall conduct either as owner or employee whether for hire or not, any game such as monte, faro, pass faro, monte rondeau, roulette, twenty-one, dice, (red and

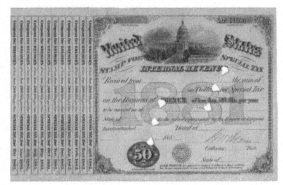

black roughet-noir), lansquenette, tan, stud horse poker, or keno, or any other game banking of whatever name, whether played with cards or dice or any other device shall be played for money, checks, credit or any other valuable thing or representative of value, the monthly license fee shall be $10." The following June, they raised that fee to $12.50.

Houses of ill fame in Tombstone, Arizona, had two types of licensing fees. The first one stated, "Every person or persons or proprietors engaged in keeping a house of ill fame where wines, malts, or spirituous liquors are sold by the glass or bottle shall pay a monthly license fee of $20." If the house of ill fame did not sell liquor, the monthly fee was reduced to $7.

When the amended ordinances were posted, many citizens were panicked and outraged. The city council and the local papers reminded people that the same reaction resulted when the ordinance was first passed in 1881. Once citizens were advised Tombstone's ordinances were similar to those in Virginia City and Los Angeles, their fears and protests quieted.

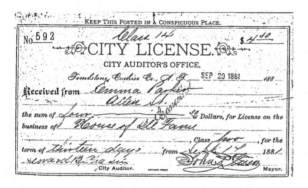

It was well known that the heart of Tombstone's business district was found on Allen Street, between and Third and Sixth Streets, but there was also a large number of businesses situated on Fremont Street. The business district was supposed to have been on Fremont, but the most successful and popular businesses found their way to Allen. A business could really be set up anywhere, except for certain ones that were not allowed in the business district. The city council passed an ordinance stating anyone could legally operate a house or room of ill-fame or prostitution, so long as they paid the proper license fees and were in the proper location. The proper location, specifically spelled out, wove around the popular business district. It began at the southern part of Tombstone, on Eighth Street, and traveled there, 150 feet north of Allen. It then paralleled Allen to Sixth, back down to Allen half way, traveled along Allen to Fifth Street until it reached Toughnut. It then went west on Toughnut until it reached Third, then traveled north, fifty feet above Allen, then west paralleling Allen to First Street.

The restriction ordinance didn't last very long, and houses of ill-fame or prostitution were allowed anywhere in Tombstone. Outraged by the lack of ordinance enforcement, a woman sent a letter to the editor of the *Epitaph*. She wrote, "It seems from your issue of the 9th that the city fathers have extended in the *demimonde* the liberties of the city. Allen Street was virtually theirs, to such an extent that a respectable woman would hesitate to even cross it. But this was not enough. Hitherto, although it has been impossible to pass along the streets provided with sidewalks without our ears being stunned with a multitude of oaths 'at every turn,' we have at least been allowed certain limits for a retired house where little children could run and play without danger of such contamination .... Is it possible there are not righteous men left to save the city? Where are all the churches and their pastors? Are they, too, joined to the cowboy element, or are they with closed eyes and ears descending upon the wickedness of King Ahab and lamenting the fall of Sodom and Gomorrah? May we not at least petition this august body to define certain limits to restrict the respectable people, if they are so sadly in the minority?" The letter was signed simply, "A Mother."

If the rules were colorful, their enforcers flamboyant. Sheriffs in many towns of the Old West earned a percentage of all taxes and fees they collected as part of their salary. This encouraged them to enforce the rules zealously and occasionally to abuse them for personal benefit. Worse, most new towns did not have established judiciaries or, often, experienced judges and lawyers to make sure justice was carried out according to the law. All of this meant that in most young towns, there was a lot of leeway.

Judge William C. Heacock reigned over court in Albuquerque, New Mexico, in the late 1800s, and he knew all about leeway. His wife, Mrs. William C. Heacock, recalled this story: Judge William C. Heacock and his cronies were playing three-card monte in the back room of a saloon. The cards were against the Judge that evening and along about one in the morning, he found himself without funds to continue his game. As was customary with the Judge in such critical situations, he called in his deputies who were drinking at the bar in the next room.

> **Sheriffs in many towns of the Old West earned a percentage of all taxes and fees they collected as part of their salary.**

"Get me a drunk," he ordered, "a drunk with money in his pockets who is guilty of disorderly conduct."

The deputies departed on their familiar mission, and the Judge retired to the courtroom on the upper floor, where he prepared to hold a session of night court. A town like Albuquerque needed a night court to keep it in order. Before long the deputies returned, carrying a limp man between them. "What the Hell?" said the Judge. "What's that you got?" "Your Honor," replied one of the deputies, as he straightened up from placing his burden on the floor, "we found him in the back room of the Blue Indigo." "Can he stand trial or is he dead drunk?" asked the Judge. "He's not drunk, but he's dead all right. He croaked himself over there in the Blue Indigo. The proprietor insisted that we get him out of there." The Judge was annoyed.

"Didn't the fools ever hear of an inquest?" he asked. He had sent for a lucrative drunk, not a drooling suicide.

He turned solemnly to his deputies. "This court is a court of justice," he said. "The right of habeas corpus must not be ignored. The prisoner must be given a speedy and fair trial. This court is ready to hear evidence. What is the charge?" "Your Honor," spoke one of the deputies. "The charge has not yet been determined." "This court will hear no case without a charge. Did you search the prisoner?" "There was a letter to some dame ..." began the deputy. "Any money?" The deputy counted $27.32. "Any weapons?" They took a gun from the hip pocket. "Has the prisoner anything to say before sentence is imposed upon him?"

Judge Heacock inclined his ear expectantly toward the prone prisoner. "In view of the unresponsiveness of the prisoner which this court interprets as contempt, and in view of the unlawful possession of a lethal weapon, this court imposes a fine of $20 and court costs," pronounced the Judge. "You might as well leave him there till morning," said the Judge as he pocketed the money. The monte game continued on the floor below.

Albuquerque wasn't the only town with questionable law practices. When Bert Mendenhall spoke of pioneer life in Portland, Oregon, in the mid 1880s, he said: "When I began the practice of law I was in my brother Ed's office .... My brother turned over little cases to us to start us off, such as those in the justice courts. We couldn't understand why we lost 'em all—every damned one. We couldn't imagine what was wrong. Well, of course, we weren't on to the ropes. The justice court was held in a room over a saloon, and the jury was selected by the constable, who picked 'em up in the saloon downstairs. All the jurors got was a dollar. Jack Evers kept the saloon. The jury would go into deliberation in a little room back of the court. There was a window in the little room, and the jurors had a gallon can with a rope tied to the bail. They would put their money in the

"Hanging Judge Roy Bean" held court in his saloon in west Texas.

bucket or can and then lower it out the window and knock it against the back door of the saloon. Then the barkeep would come out, peek in the bucket to see if there was any money, and if there was, it was o.k., he'd send it up full of beer or whatever they wanted. Then the jury would come to an agreement, but what they agreed on depended on which side furnished the money for the bucket. Once there was a state case involving a criminal charge. The jury was pretty full that time. It brought in a verdict that read, 'State guilty as charged.' It was about '84 or '85 that there was a justice court out on Ninth and Glisan streets, where the front room was the bar and the rear room with a side entrance, the place for holding court. The justice of the peace owned the place, and the barkeeper was the constable."

Not every lawman was a gambler on the side. In Wichita Falls, Texas, a man named Nat Henderson took on the betting interests and triumphed—at least for a while. "I was county surveyor for a while.

I ran for county attorney in 1896 and was elected. It was against the law for there to be any public gambling, but it went on just the same. The sheriff and his men were in with the gamblers, and they had a regular gambling hall. I had been gambling some, and when I was elected county attorney they told me they were all right then as I gambled and they didn't think I would enforce the law. I told 'em I wasn't going to gamble anymore and they had to quit, too. But when I got in office and tried to enforce the law, I soon found I was at loggerheads with the sheriff and his department. I couldn't do a thing toward enforcing the law against gambling, and it went right on. There was a little man with the nerve of Bill McDonald who was a deputy sheriff. His name was Sam Abbott. He and the sheriff got at outs and the sheriff put him off the force. Sam came to me, and he said if I could get him an official position, we could clean up the gambling. I got him on as deputy constable. We cleaned up the gambling and there wasn't any gambling to speak of here for several years."

Another Texas town proved tough for one saloonkeeper and the town sheriff. J. L. Tarter lived in Fort Worth during the 1880s. He remembered this story: "One of the first real tests the city officials had to face was in a matter with Ed Rosoux, who came to Taylor from Bastrop County. He opened a saloon in Taylor and was building up a good business. Rosoux would not allow anyone to take a person out of his saloon if the person was drunk. He was a native of Kentucky and came to Taylor with a reputation of being tough. He had killed a couple men in Bastrop County. However, he was an elegant looking man and carried along with his fighting ability, intelligence and polished manners."

Tarter continued, "There came a time when the officers wanted a man against whom there was some misdemeanor charge. Deputy constable Morris was handed the warrant to execute. The party wanted was drunk and in Rosoux's saloon. Deputy Morris entered the saloon and led the man out of the door before Rosoux happened to notice what was taking place. When Rousoux realized what the deputy was doing, he stepped to the door quickly and demanded that the person be turned loose. Morris refused to comply with the demand and Rosoux, without further words, hit the deputy on the jaw, knocking him into the ditch. Rosoux then took the drunk back into the saloon. When Rosoux's act was reported to the Mayor, he issued a warrant promptly for the arrest of Rosoux. Tom Smith served the warrant on Smith, but let him go on Rosoux's own recognizance. The trial was called in Mayor Moody's court. The city attorney presented the city's evidence and then the Mayor called the defendant to present his evidence. When Rosoux arose to his feet and made a short speech to the court, which was as follows: 'So far as this Kangaroo Court is concerned, it can go to hell.' Following his speech, Rosoux walked out of the court and returned to his saloon. Rosoux's action toward the Mayor's court tightened the position considerable and things became tense. There was a citation issued for Rosoux to appear instantly and answer to a charge of contempt of court. With a charge of assault and battery and interfering with an officer standing against Rosoux, in addition the contempt citation, the officers were compelled to take charge of the man. Tom Smith was given the papers to serve and take Rosoux in custody. With Rosoux having the reputation for being one of the best shots in the state, and there was no doubt about his courage, and Tom Smith with an equal reputation, the people were all set to see a high-class gun fight. When Tom Smith started for Rosoux's saloon to arrest him, Smith had an audience of citizens who wanted to see how good their marshal was with the gun and the amount of his courage. Smith entered the saloon and found Rosoux playing. He walked up to Rosoux and said: 'Rosoux, I've come to talk with you a bit.' 'That you may do to your own satisfaction, start talking,' he invited.

"'Well, you have made bad matters worse by walking out on the court. I have come here to suggest that you and I go to the court and see if the situation can be fixed up.' 'Smith, I am not going with you or any other man to satisfy that bunch of kangaroo jobers,' was Rosoux's reply. 'I advise you to do so, Rosoux,' Smith pleaded, 'because it's things like this that lead to gunplay.' 'When I get ready to pop you shall know it, and if you don't stop molesting me it will not be long,' Rosoux stated while he laid the pool cue down. 'I am ready now,' Smith replied, and at the same instance he fired his gun at Rosoux. The bullet entered his side, but he leaped over his bar, quick as a flash, and drew his gun. He fired, but dropped to the floor while shooting and died in a short time afterwards. Rosoux had a great number of friends. They felt that Smith took advantage of the saloon man. That feeling was the reason for Smith's defeat at the following election. Willis Johnson was elected, and that defeat injured Smith's pride considerable."

Conclusion

Whether it was drinking, gambling, or some other type of "sin," vice played an integral role in the West's expansion.

As people left their Eastern homes for a piece of the Western pie, their reasons were as varied as the people themselves. Some felt too constricted in proper towns and wanted the freedom of open space. Some saw a chance to own land and become successful business owners. Others were either running from a past or got gold fever and gambled everything for a chance to get rich.

The trek out West in itself was a gamble—lack of water, hostile Indians, bad weather, and a shortage of supplies were just some of the risks involved. Once there, many had no idea what to expect or what they may encounter. Even Wyatt Earp, who arrived in Tombstone with the intent of beginning a stage line, was forced to come up with a new plan, because when he arrived, he found two successful stage lines already in operation. Going West meant taking your chances.

It's easy to understand why vices such as drinking and gambling were so popular. With towns suddenly springing up in bare patches of land, most saloons weren't built because men were alcoholics—well, some were—but they served as social gathering places where lonely men kept other lonely men company. They could easily have been called a men's club since most met there to read papers, smoke cigars, talk politics, and gamble. Yes, of course, they sold liquor, but it was enjoyed with conversation and cigars.

Most of the men who owned or worked in the saloons were highly respected in their towns. In fact, the saloon owner was often privy to a multitude of conversations and sometimes even possibly influenced the outcome of business or political decisions. Saloonkeepers must certainly have contributed to the success of a town. Their business license fees and taxes alone helped support the town's budget.

Being a gambler was also a highly respected profession, at least in some circles. Gambling was business, and the men who participated took it seriously. It's easy to understand why men got shot for cheating at cards. If a man made his living at gambling, a cheater could have cost him his livelihood.

Men became gamblers for a variety of reasons. Some weren't skilled at anything else, while others liked the thrill of living of the edge. Still others, like Doc Holliday, were forced into it. He started out as a professional dentist in Georgia, but when he got tuberculosis, his doctor recommended he head West. He tried hanging out a dental shingle, but it soon failed. Who wanted a sick, coughing dentist? He turned to the only other option he had—gambling.

Miners, businessmen, and cowhands also gambled, but it was merely for entertainment. After working all day or night, they wanted to unwind. Often, in most newly formed remote towns, gambling was the only resort. For a man coming off a cattle drive or out of a dark mine, walking into a saloon or billiard hall and plunking down some coins or gold dust must have seemed like entering a glittering casino does to us today. What fun!

While men were content to visit with one another in a saloon or gambling hall, they also longed for female companionship. Enter the prostitute. Whether she chose to enter the business willingly, or was forced into it to support herself, the men were happy to see her.

Most newly formed towns consisted of men only—even Tombstone, Arizona, was nicknamed "Stagtown" for a while. In most towns' early stages, prostitutes weren't scorned—they were welcomed. They weren't scorned until after the towns began to grow and "proper" women either arrived with, or to join, their husbands. Once this happened, prostitutes were forced to live in certain sections of towns to avoid the regular folk. Not all prostitutes felt the need to do this, and they blatantly walked the streets proper, just to stir things up a bit!

The Wicked West

While most people out West felt their lifestyles were acceptable, others did not. Easterners—and some Westerners—felt these vices were the work of the devil himself. It is true that many became alcoholics, drug addicts, and murderers, but not everyone did.

Those facts didn't matter to the people advocating temperance. The movement hit the West hard, and at its core. Since many smaller towns didn't have a theater or social club, the only entertainment they had was a saloon or gambling hall. Eventually with the Temperance movement, coupled with the flood of people moving West and "civilizing" the life there, gambling and prostitution were outlawed in most places, and saloons struggled to survive. By the turn of the century, the West was struggling with new technology, and the way of life was changed forever. The price of silver plummeted and mining was brought to its knees, while train cars were being loaded with cattle that once walked the "trail."

Could the West have been expanded and developed without all these vices? Maybe, but what a boring place it would have been!

Acknowledgments and Sources

Writing a book is like building a house ... it can't be done alone. Having said that, I would like to thank the following people for making this book possible:

My husband, Larry—his unwavering support, honest critiques, and sense of humor keep me going.

My editors, Ed Finn, Teresa Kennedy, and Lisa Cooper—their thoroughness, creativity, enthusiasm, and easy working style made this book sparkle.

Ron M. James, Nevada's State Historic Preservation Officer, for all the wonderful data and insights into Virginia City's wild past.

Rio Nuevo Publishers for having the insight and faith to publish my book.

The majority of the quoted material in this book came from the Library of Congress, Manuscript Division, W.P.A. Federal Writers' Project Collection, Washington, D.C. Recipes for popular mixed drinks in the Wild West came from *Harry Johnson's Bartenders' Manual*, 1882.

PHOTO CREDITS AS FOLLOWS: Objects pictured on pages 25, 73, 80, and 122 (photographed by Robin Stancliff) appear courtesy of Marge and Steve Elliot, from the collection of the Tombstone Western Heritage Museum, 519 East Fremont Street, Tombstone, Arizona, 85638; 520-457-3800. • Photos on front cover and on pages 12, 31, 44, 64, 66, 74, 81, 104, 130, and 133 courtesy of the Library of Congress. • Images on pages 39, 55, and 143 from the private collection of Sherry Monahan. • Photo on page 76 courtesy of the South Dakota State Historical Society–State Archives. • Photo on page 98: with thanks to the Bob Hope Private Collection. • Photo on page 106: with thanks to Americans.net/Outlaw Women. • Image on page 144 courtesy of Arizona Historical Society. • Photo on page 148 was taken circa 1900 by Lippe Studio, Del Rio, Texas.

Suggested Reading

Finn, Ed. *The Legend of the O.K. Corral*. Tucson, AZ: Rio Nuevo Publishers, 2005.

James, Ronald M. *The Roar and the Silence: A History of Virginia City and the Comstock Lode*. Reno, NV: University of Nevada Press, 1998.

Lindstrom, Stan, and Wynn Lindstrom, eds. *Gold, Gals, Guns, Guts: A History of Deadwood, Lead, and Spearfish, 1874–1976*. Pierre, SD: South Dakota State Historical Society Press, 2004.

Levy, Jo Ann. *They Saw the Elephant: Women in the California Gold Rush*. Norman, OK: University of Oklahoma Press, 1992.

Monahan, Sherry. *Taste of Tombstone: A Hearty Helping of History*. Ravia, OK: Royal Spectrum Publishing, 1998.

Twain, Mark (Smith, Harriet Elinor, and Edgar Marquess Branch, eds.). *Roughing It*. Berkeley, CA: University of California Press, 2003.

Also recommended: *True West* magazine.

Index

INDEX

INDEX

INDEX